The Politics
of National Security

THE POLITICS
OF
NATIONAL
SECURITY

Marcus G. Raskin

Transaction Books
New Brunswick, New Jersey

Library of Congress Catalog Number: 77-55935
ISBN: 0-87855-239-1 (cloth); 0-87855-662-1 (paper)
Printed in the United States of America

Library of Congress Cataloging in Publication Data
Raskin, Marcus G.
   National security.

   Includes bibliographical references and index.
   1. National security. 2. United States—National security. 3.
United States—Foreign economic relations. I. Title.
UA10.5.R37   327.73   77-55935
ISBN 0-87855-239-1
ISBN 0-87855-662-1 pbk.

To our dear friend and colleague,
Sam Rubin

Contents

Acknowledgements

This book grew out of a series of discussions with my colleague, Bob Borosage. To him I owe a special debt of gratitude. Ann Wilcox, my gifted assistant, worked with dedication and a critical eye to what she read.

I want to acknowledge my deep appreciation to my colleagues Richard Barnet, Saul Landau, Ralph Stavins, Trin Yarborough, Martha Graff, and Pat Goldstein. Ronni Karpen Moffitt helped me in an early stage. She was taken from us with our colleague Orlando Letelier in a political assassination in September of 1976.

I wish to thank the members of the Institute for Policy Studies and donors to it—the Samuel Rubin Foundation, Janss Foundation, the Bydale Foundation and the Laras Foundation—who have supported us in developing studies of the national security state.

Books are always difficult on families, especially where various of the family members are writing multiple volumes. I hope that Erika, Jamie, Noah, and Barbara Raskin will find things in this book that will help them to inquire further into this last period of our history. Finally, I wish to thank Irving Louis Horowitz and Scott Bramson of Transaction Books, and Alice Mayhew of Simon and Schuster for her patience.

1
The New Fit

In 1973 men whose economic and political interests transcended those of any political party, who meet in private clubs like the Links club of New York or the Metropolitan club of Washington, began talking about the need to find a presidential candidate who could master the populist stance without actually being populist. Their ideal type was a man whose personal style would not become a public embarrassment, and who would give the appearance of accessibility. In addition, the ideal candidate would have learned Gene McCarthy's manner of going directly to the people with a cause, (albeit the ambiguous one of sincerity) and would not challenge the dominant U.S. corporations, the banks, the modern national security apparatus, or those governmental agencies and elites friendly to these institutions.

Their task was an urgent one for the reason that the terrible war which they had once strongly supported was winding down. By 1973 they were undercutting its purpose through their dissent and distaste for then President Richard Nixon. Nixon was haranguing them with a most astonishing idea: they

1

had lost the will to govern. So here was Nixon with a group of arriviste millionaires including C. Arnholt Smith, Bebe Rebozo, Clement Stone, and White House operators like John Ehrlichman, and Bob Halderman, all seeking to set their own terms for the operations of the state and of corporations through centralization of power in the hands of this new group. These pretenders frightened the old oligarchs[1] in the same way that Senator Joe McCarthy had frightened the CIA and the army some twenty years before. McCarthy, bored with hunting dentists as communists, had extended his domain to include generals and upper class officials in the CIA, men protected and nurtured by the oligarchs. They had destroyed McCarthy politically under the kleig lights of television. The same destruction occurred in Nixon's case. The old oligarchs saw their chance when Nixon dithered and faltered by not burning the tapes or acting with cruelty and dispatch against his many adversaries, including the head of IBM. Nixon was thus destroyed by the televised hearings of the Watergate Committee.

Once Nixon had lost the presidency, partly because he surrounded himself with those who knew the price of everything and the value of nothing, while he knew the value of everything but could not figure out anyone's price, the question soon arose whether those who had initiated the Vietnam War and later slinked off to law firms, corporations, and universities could again return to political power without having to operate through surrogates. It is said that after a war is lost, those who lose that war cannot, in the short term, expect to politically survive its loss. They are required to give way to a new elite divorced from the war and its failure. At first it appeared that the men who served as the initiators of the Vietnam War would not be able to return to power. As it turned out, however, it was Nixon, then Ford and Kissinger who watched their ambassador, Graham Martin, scramble out of Vietnam with those who served the U.S. expeditionary force. Nixon and Ford were tagged the losers and those who initiated the war could reinstate themselves several years later. One is reminded here of the German general staff at the end of the First World War which made sure that it was not the Junker generals who surrendered to the Allies but Junker-manipulated soldier councils and the civilian Social Democrats.

Even after Nixon resigned, the tantalizing question persisted whether it was possible for those who reneged in their war in Indochina to return to power without reformation or repentance. Was there a way to keep intact the state apparatus which had been so carefully crafted since 1941 by the old oligarchs? For these purposes, they needed to find a legitimate but relatively obscure candidate who talked morality and economy and had a healthy empirical respect for the social order in the sense of knowing where real power lay in the society. He would have to be a man who could restore allegiance to the old system and know how to coopt liberal forces which otherwise might overturn the entire checkerboard. They did not want Fred Harris for this task. He was too much like George McGovern who had surfaced in 1972 to win the Democratic nomination by capturing local caucuses. McGovern claimed that the Democratic Party with his guidance would end the Vietnam War, cut the defense budget, and make liberal-populist inroads in the economic system. He won nomination through vigorous local campaigning at the grass roots level. The old oligarchs had thought in 1971–72 that it would be enough to give their public endorsement to their candidate Ed Muskie and that the people would then automatically follow their choice. Nixon's dirty tricks and Muskie's own ineptitude however, thwarted the oligarchs. They needed someone who could play the right-left populist game of Wallace and Harris.

Then came ambitious and hard-working Jimmy Carter from Plains, Georgia, with a tenacious will and a readiness to do what was necessary to line up the forces of social change in support of the old order. He achieved this recognition by using his disregard of pomp, his good sense, and diligence to demonstrate that he had the vital trait common to most presidents of the United States: missionary zeal. Jimmy Carter was hungry, and the established forces appreciate the hungry, the ambitious, and those who have what Edmund Wilson called "formidable tenacity of character." Although the old oligarchs are publicly appalled at the antics of a self-promoter, they privately admire such a person and believe that he can almost always be used for their purpose even when his actions become coercive.

Sometimes, of course, political leaders get out of hand and do not respect the fiefdoms or the debts owed to the oligarchs. Bertrand Russell noted that gifted political men often use the rich for their own purposes. "Caesar was helped to power by his creditors who had no hope of repayment except through his success; but when he succeeded he was powerful enough to defy them. Charles V borrowed from the Fuggers the money required to buy the position of Emperor . . . when he became Emperor he snapped his fingers at them and they lost what they had."[2]

But for the time being we find that David Rockefeller, our modern Crassus, was rewarded by having at least fifteen of his ambitious Trilateral Commission members named to the highest government and cabinet positions. Some of the more astute members of the commission especially Andrew Young, had advanced ideas which he tested for the oligarchs and the state in the U.N. Young took the line that America should not interrupt radical change in foreign countries because the United States was economically and militarily powerful enough to turn any such changes to its own advantage. He noted that cold and hot war antagonists sought aid and trade with the United States, thereby increasing its power and world authority. Zbigniew Brzezinski, the chief of staff of the Trilateral Commission before becoming a presidential adviser, had long argued that the United States did not mobilize its obvious advantages economically and politically in the third world and in Eastern Europe. Such ideas could only strengthen large corporate power.

Like Brzezinski, Carter was neither frightened by the use of military power nor transfixed by it. He was the first president to ride the command plane which a president uses to direct nuclear war fighting. He judged the Soviets to be weak and accepted Brzezinski's argument that the Soviets feared the Chinese and the non-Russian Soviet population which comprised 50 percent of the total population. He devoutly believed that this second 50 percent of the population was in search of its own national self-identity. The tight national security group around Carter, Harold Brown, Brzezinski, Schlesinger, Vance, and Turner of the CIA believed that the strength of the Soviet Union which touched on the United States and its interests concerned only strategic armaments (an area of arms in which the Soviets are able to deter a first strike attack by the United States).

The first U.S. proposals on strategic arms limitation, crafted by the the Department of Defense and Senator Jackson, were calculated to limit the Soviet deterrent without affecting the strategic capability of the United States. Carter's new policies toward the USSR on fishing rights, human rights, SALT, trade, and radio propaganda stemmed from the recognition of U.S. financial and economic primacy, the Baptist ideology of goodness and purpose, skepticism of Soviet ideological appeal, and their military strength.

In practice, the changes in U.S. foreign and national security policy since Ford, Rockefeller, and Nixon are very refined ones. These changes are best symbolized by the political eclipse of Nelson Rockefeller, the oligarch defense buff, and by the political emergence of his oligarch-banker brother David Rockefeller, who believed the financial community can rely on indirect modes of economic control rather than on costly defense systems and little wars to retain U.S. primacy. David Rockefeller's point of view requires the protection of the U.S. dollar as the world's standard of exchange and measure in international markets. These goals are however, hard to achieve without a measure of arms control. The Warnke-Vance wing of the administration would like the Soviet Union to join the United States in bilateral arms control because the United States has long had an imperial defense system which is outmoded, expensive, and untranslatable into usable power. The costly international defense system of the United States is seen to weaken the dollar. Liberal members of the Carter administration hope that the Soviets will rescue the United States from the inertia of the arms acquisition process. The major question which the Soviets face is whether they are prepared to enter into arms control agreements with the United States in order to stop the United States from doing that which it should not have undertaken in the first place. This was the hope of Secretary Vance, Carter's most prudent advisor.

It is not accidental that the cabinet appointees to the Department of Treasury, Commerce, and State have been involved directly with multinational corporations and are recent IBM board members. Corporations like IBM emerge as central actors with dual roles during the 1940s. They offered their sophisticated computers to defense, intelligence, and other security agencies; they built the calculative infrastructure of the national security state. Yet they remained private and stayed independent of the state by becoming multi-centered world corporations with their own interests and "foreign policies." Predictably, the corporations which blossomed during the post-World War II imperial thrust are now considered more important, more fashionable, and even more useful to the state bureaucracy. Brzezinski, one of the bureaucracy's "global planners," made the following statement to the Murphy Commission:

> What impresses me generally in foreign affairs is that modern large scale, internationally active corporations have a far more effective way of operating internationally than the State Department. I would much rather deal with the representatives of IBM than with many of our embassies, in terms of perspicacity of analysis, flexibility of operations and rapidity of movements.[3]

When Brzezinski described IBM in these glowing terms he was, in fact, underlining the next phase of

U.S. foreign policy. In rhetorical terms, this position was similar to that of the State Department prior to World War II: the United States should always lead with its economic power rather than its military power and should exercise tight controls over arms shipments.

Because U.S. multinational corporation trade is $400 billion per year, the Carter administration has sought a more conscious integration of U.S. international capitalism and national state power so as to help the great U.S. corporations retain their prime share of world markets. Some bureaucrats and business elites grumbled that Kissinger failed to confront economic policy issues and help business. Despite complaints from big business about Kissinger's lack of economic interest, the Rockefellers thought enough of his economic acumen to make him vice-chairman of Chase Manhattan Bank's international investment committee in 1977. Kissinger had attempted to shift the focus of U.S. diplomacy from a military to an economic one. But this task was especially hard to accomplish as secretary of state because of the militarization of U.S. foreign policy during the entire cold war period, the Indochina war, and Kissinger's own fascination with weaponry and war fighting.

Like past presidents, Carter chose men and women for his cabinet whose personal success was related to the emergence of the United States as a world empire, the expansion of the role of the national state (especially its security aspects), and the growth of the decentered global corporation (a legal entity dependent on the use of U.S. dollars as a currency that all foreigners will accept and hold). The previous government experience of men like state and defense secretaries Cyrus Vance and Harold Brown was directly linked to the imperial role of the United States and especially the logistical bureaucratic support necessary to keep that apparatus operating.

Carter's cabinet appointments symbolized the restoration of the war initiators. These appointments were given to those who approved, planned, or embraced the Indochina War. One of them, Joe Califano, helped to coin the hideous phrase, "body count," to describe the Vietnamese dead after a search and destroy mission when he was an adviser in the Defense Department. Such people, although they recognize the war as an economic miscalculation, were never public opponents of the war. Instead, they retreated into silence or dinner party dissent after Johnson left the presidency.

Eight years later at his confirmation hearings for the position of secretary of state, Vance, who had served as Johnson's negotiator at the Paris talks with the North Vietnamese in 1968, wondered why the United States bothered with such an adventure. The favorable business and investment arrangements which the Vietnamese offered world corporations within two years after the war affirmed a pragmatic belief that the war was a political error from the U.S. standpoint because it did not require a military solution. The North Vietnamese were open to becoming a market for U.S. goods and to economic development with U.S. advice.

For Carter, himself a supporter of the war, the ten-year tragedy was a mistake only to the extent that its social cost exceeded the domestic political price U.S. leaders could afford to pay for the war's continuation.

Carter's policies toward the Soviet Union have been a series of probing exercises. He has aggressively tested its leadership with contradictory proposals. His expert on Eastern Europe-Soviet relations, Zbigniew Brzezinski was the critical actor in Soviet-U.S. relations in the administration's initial stages. It should be noted that Brzezinski favored the Indochina War and bombing the Cuban missile sites in 1962. Unlike Kissinger, who saw the United States as a status quo role fighting a rear guard battle for western civilization, Brzezinski holds that the United States is a revolutionary nation and that it need not be defensive in world affairs if it forges a grand vision. The strategy of this grand vision is meant to cause dissension within Eastern Europe and the Soviet Union. Brzezinski's assumption is that there is little cost to the United States even if this strategy fails since the Soviets are weak in any case.[4] Furthermore, the United States has the option of changing its stand towards the Soviet Union as long as the attacks on the Soviet Union only cause bad moods in its leadership.

Polish emigrés like Brzezinski, see Poland as part of "western civilization." To them, Poland is a country which, with modest help from Western Europe, can withstand both communism and the Soviet Union. They see Soviets as suspended in the land of purgatory between Asia and the West. This mindset translates politically and diplomatically into a position that was followed against the Soviet Union after World War I. At that time, Germany, France, England, as well as the United States, believed Poland and other states in Eastern Europe such as Romania and Czechoslovakia were critical to the policy of establishing the *cordon sanitaire* around the revolutionary fervor emanating from the Soviet Union. The *cordon sanitaire* position is still present in the thinking of this and other national security advisors.[5]

One instrument of the grand vision is human rights. President Carter's administration hoped to recapture the world image of moral champion (not unlike the sermonizing of Woodrow Wilson) while continuing the same imperial mischief. Its political objective was to split Soviet elites within the Communist Party and within its bureaucratic and scientific apparatus. There was another internal salving purpose. The trauma of the Indochina War left an ugly scar to be hidden from the American people, the national security bureaucracy, and the rest of the world. U.S. officials in the Carter administration used the human rights issue as a device to mask the policies and devastating results of that war. Raising human rights as an issue has also given Carter some flexibility by allowing him to limit or moderate international commitments to leaders and alliance systems adjudged politically shaky or unpopular. Through using a scorecard on human rights, the United States can actively reconsider its various alliance systems with the critical exception of NATO.

Brzezinski's grand vision includes the vectoring of Eastern Europe to Western Europe through trade arrangements and skillful armament and disarmament proposals. This vectoring will isolate, in his terms, the geriatric and inflexible Soviet bureaucracy and leadership from the Soviet people. When we seek to understand the attitudes of the Carter administration toward the Soviet Union, it is well to remember Brzezinski's awareness of Eastern European history, (a history easily overlooked by many Americans). After the Second World War, Stalin's intention in extending control over Poland was related to events which occurred during the Russian Civil War of 1919-20. At that time, Stalin supported the advance of Soviet troops to the suburbs of Warsaw under the Soviet commander Tutkatchevski. However, the Polish commander, General Pilsudski, called on the French for military aid. With French assistance, the Poles defeated the Soviet forces who retreated to Minsk. After the Second World War, Stalin believed that it was necessary to finish old business in Poland and return Poland to the Soviet sphere of influence. This included installing in Warsaw the communist-oriented Lublin Poles, a government friendly to the Russians. Stalin did not intend to be denied a victory that the Bolsheviks a generation earlier had decided was necessary for their security. Therefore, in 1944 he refused to support the Warsaw uprising which he feared could turn against the Soviet troops in ways similar to the events of 1920. The British and Americans accepted Stalin's position, and anti-Soviet Poles saw this acceptance as a betrayal.

Such reevaluations and policy shifts encased in preachy and moralistic language in no way impair the inexorable character of the thirty-five-year-old national security bureaucracy that continues to produce plans for war, semi-war, covert operations, shows of force, and new weapons systems. These plans are always seductively available for implementation if a presidential party falters in using its economic tools to achieve world primacy. On the other hand, Carter's policy makers are skeptical of the national security bureaucracy because of its inflexibility. They do not quite know how or whether to change the mission of four million bureaucrats whose sole task is the production of anticommunism and imperial offense. This production takes the form of plans for actual capabilities for first strike, larger ground forces, greater reliance on weapons research, military assistance, and plans for direct and indirect domination. One reason for this development is that part of Carter's presidential group operates on these assumptions. Thus, James Schlessinger's view on defense and national security matters remained the fundamental one that the bureaucracy actually uses as its guide in daily operations. It is one to which Harold Brown, due to the nature of his work, pledged himself.

There is little chance that the alliance system will end or be changed. The Carter administration has inherited the fantasy that 500,000 U.S. troops are stationed abroad because the United States has legal commitments which it is required to defend militarily. In reality, the treaties are written in such a way that the United States has no military commitment to the various nations except in case of attack and then only in terms of its constitutional processes.[6] If the United States were to remove its military presence from these various countries, it would mean that the U.S. bureaucracy, corporations, and military were prepared to allow each of the forty-two nations involved to operate according to its own purposes and to be open to internal social transformation. What would those four million people in the military and national security establishment do if they did not prepare for a simultaneous strategic nuclear and nonnuclear war in different parts of the world? The consequence is that U.S. strategic and nonnuclear forces are arming at a faster pace than that which occurred under Nixon, although the startling U.S. cost of the arms race ($160 billion by 1980) has caused some, like Brzezinski, to say that only "poor and backward nations can afford" to have a war.[7] Nevertheless, an arms control agreement which destroyed future development of weapons and a defense industrial plant is economically and politically unpopular. The South and Southwest, Carter's cultural home, have gained much economic and political status from the arms race, and even from the Indochina War. In addition, there is little to suggest that the military-minded wing of the Democratic Party with its strength in Congress and other cold-war allies including the AFL-CIO leadership will allow the arms acquisition process to lessen in intensity especially if it means a cut in future arms development and loss of jobs.

Carter's less bellicose contingent, including Anthony Lake, assistant secretary of state for policy planning, Les Gelb, Paul Warnke, Cyrus Vance, and James Leonard, deputy representative to the U.N., know that they are thought to be woolly-headed by Schlesinger supporters such as Dean Rusk, Paul Nitze, Eugene Rostow, and Charls Walker. Schlesinger's supporters have started a Committee on the Present Danger to counteract any policy changes in the U.S. cold war posture, making sure that the rhetoric of nuclear or conventional disarmament does not become a reality, and that the loss in Vietnam does not radically change U.S. strategies. Vice-president Mondale's early meetings with NATO officials strengthened greatly the hand of those in the bureaucracy who see military weaponry and troops as the glue of alliance and U.S. hegemony thus strengthening in the bureaucracy the older cold warrior position. This position is reenforced by Senator Nunn (Georgia) and other congressional leaders, notably Stennis of Mississippi and Moynihan (New York) who throughout the 95th Congress sought to increase

U.S. troops to NATO even if an agreement would have been reached with the Soviet Union on strategic arms.

Studies by Henry Owen of the NSC and Barry Blechman, an administration arms control adviser, outline this "need." Such studies do not manifest a conscious wish to engage in major war. However, they provide the intellectual policy sustenance for war preparations, military maneuvers, and projects that show military power without direct military engagement. This imperial concept was once called "showing the flag." The political purpose which the presence of troops serves in advanced industrial countries is similar to its role in poor nations.

Those who support the U.S. military beefing-up in Western Europe are concerned that as Western Europe unifies and turns to the Left flirting with a strong parliamentary coalition of social democrats, communists, and socialists, the United States will be required to increase its non-nuclear military presence in order to affect and shape the internal politics of Western Europe. The NATO charter appears to allow for internal interference if such actions can be rationalized in the context of a threat to peace and the claim of external aggression. In fact centrist coalitions proved more durable than Left organizing in Europe. But the dialectics of military politics are such as to strengthen the intentions of those who want to increase U.S. forces in Europe because they represent American military vitality.

Nevertheless, the Carter cabinet would like to control defense spending to a 9.5 per year increase (6 percent for inflation) and locate generals and admirals who know the value of a dollar and are satisfied with the indirect use of force. They would like to extend the "deputy" system of diplomacy in which Egypt is expected to do its bidding in Africa just as Iran is expected to operate for the United States in the Middle East. This is the purpose of the U.S. military assistance program. Paradoxically, these instruments are gauged to conservative internal spending policies and the need to stabilize the world currency system around the U.S. dollar. Like Eisenhower, Carter believes that an imperial presence in the world requires internal stability and an economic policy which produces a noninflation dollar that is more solid than gold. Carter's economic advisors, Charles Schultze and Michael Blumenthal, believe that this mode of economic stability requires the rejection of new government spending programs that would, in their view, cause inflation. There is also a political component to their view. They fear that spending would politically excite the poor and deprived to make unmanageable demands on the U.S. economic system which could not be met in the context of present modes of capitalism.

U.S. leaders who concern themselves with world military plans often wonder whether the United States can afford the alliance system without more economic payoff control. Nixon's treasury secretary, John Connally, made the following statement to the American Bankers Association in 1971:

> Financing a military shield is part of the burden of leadership; the responsibilities cannot and should not be cast off. But twenty-five years after World War II, legitimate questions arise over how the cost of these responsibilities should be allocated among the free-world allies who benefit from that shield. The nations of Western Europe and Japan are again strong and vigorous, and their capacities to contribute have vastly in-

creased. I find it an impressive fact, and depressing fact, that the persistent underlying balance of payments deficit which causes such concern is more than covered, year in and year out, by our net military expenditures abroad, over and above amounts received from military purchases in the United States.[8]

Connally's ideas are similar to those of members of the Democratic Party including Mike Mansfield, Carter's ambassador to Japan, who as a senator held that the disengagement policy in Western Europe was of central importance in protecting the dollar and paying for new social programs in the United States.

Unlike Connally, Carter's advisors think that the United States has a far greater margin for error than the conventional, post-Vietnam policy analysts usually conclude. A number of those members of the Carter administration participated in a study published in September 1976 entitled *Principles for Defining the National Interest*. The conclusion of that public opinion study was that "in so far as foreign policy professionals determine it, our foreign policy in the period just ahead will probably be characterized by continuity far more than sudden shifts or sharp departures. Also reassuring to those who see the United States as a nation consumed by self-doubt should be the considerable overlap in professional views and public attitudes on many key issues."[9] The assumption behind this study was that a consensus can be managed for virtually any series of tactical policy moves.

The analysis of the Carter administration is grounded on three assumptions: that the United States increases its trade in markets abroad to offset the U.S. balance of payments problem; that Carter successfully restores the American self-image of goodness and idealism (as for example concerning the issue of human rights); and that the media can be muscled or hustled to support established power's interpretations of events and policies. The policies, of course, had not changed, although for a short time the leaders were whistling a different tune. One of the problems in the last decade for government officials in the national security sphere was that the media appeared to follow different facts and assumptions about governing and power. For a time, young reporters turned their eyes to questions which contradicted the established view of reality. Since 1973 men such as Dean Rusk have devoted themselves to finding ways that the military and business elites could foreclose the media from developing adverse positions to those followed in the upper reaches of the state and corporate apparatus. This situation occurred previously during the Indochina War.

Because there is belief in policy flexibility, contradictory initiatives on a rhetorical level were continued by the Carter administration. This parry and thrust tactic had the effect of confusing a bureaucracy which presents and pursues its own alternatives. This has the effect of undercutting a unified and coherent position in national security policy. However, the structural reasons for this lack of coherence go deeper than Carter's tactics. They grow out of internal economic and regional conflicts within the United States, a competing assessment of the dangers of communism, competition between military costs and the politically expressed needs of the society, the absence of a unifying national purpose that transcends competing policies and interests among ruling elites, and a split between those who believe in military force as the prime significant instrument in world affairs and those who favor economic levers as the mechanism for primacy. Because the Carter administration has no overall vision which it can politically sustain, it will settle for certain pragmatic goals such as avoiding the sort of individual mistakes and miscalculations that Carter advisors believe led to the Indochina War.

Paradoxically, these pragmatic goals can be achieved while appearing to be mistakes. One such "mistake" is being critical of all national governments and thus reaching over the heads of state in the same manner that Carter has adopted internally in reaching over the heads of Congress through town meetings and call-ins. This method seeks to make family quarrels public with the specific purpose of risking all past international arrangements with both friends and enemies. This practice is not as revolutionary as it may appear and is a classic approach to international politics. The Soviet-German rapprochement in the 1920s, and the Ribbentrop-Molotov pact serve as examples. Anglo-French detenté in the 1830s and 1840s and the German-Italian military alliance after 1935 are others. But before such national shifts occur, elites reassess their friends.

It is sometimes said that diplomacy is the history of deals struck between enemies against friends. This Machiavellian rule was practiced throughout the cold war. Of course, the public was told that the enemy was X, while in reality, the problems of the United States concerned Y. It was only under Kissinger that this rule was publicly practiced due to the chaos resulting from the Indochina War. Thus, at the time of the August 1971 devaluation of the U.S. dollar, the United States treated Japan summarily in relation to its "enemy," China. At the same time, the

Soviet Union enjoyed a greater power partnership status with the United States on issues which the allies of both nations believed were unshakeable arrangements between them. The United States had no qualms about using its leverage with oil producing countries against Western Europe when challenged by France and Germany in 1973 during the oil crisis. According to John Stoessinger, Western Europeans had charged that "their capitals had become little more than refueling stops on his [Kissinger's] way to or back from Moscow."[10]

The "adversary as friend" rule is also often used by Brzezinski and Cyrus Vance. Indeed, the United States could conclude agreements with China or the Soviet Union while relationships with the Europeans or the Japanese deteriorated just because their corporate oligarchies become more aggressive internationally. Before coming to power, Brzezinski described this possibility in the following passage:

> ... a fundamental change in the very pattern of international relations is not to be excluded. We could find a situation a decade from now in which our relations with either the Soviets or the Chinese, assuming there is no reversal in that relationships are more stable, more predictable and less pregnant with hostility than our relations with either the Europeans or the Japanese. This, indeed, would be a fundamental reversal of world affairs, one which would undo the very thrust of much of American foreign policy since World War Two.[11]

In the past, the managers of the U.S. empire have spent a considerable amount of time hiding the fact that state relations were more cordial with enemies than they were with friends. Senator Stuart

Symington discussed this point during a hearing on nuclear testing, reduction, and proliferation.

> We were told, by implication, that the country blocking information on the things that were being done was the Soviet Union, which is a participant as are France, Germany, Canada, Great Britain and ourselves. I found out that this is not true. It isn't the Soviet Union at all. They are perfectly willing to have this information come out. There is a meeting that bears on what we are talking about. Those meetings in London are the most important that have ever been held, because together those seven countries could really do something about this matter. The Soviet Union, from what I understand—I am a member of the Joint Committee on Atomic Energy—has been quite cooperative in the discussions. But another country, who for many years has made a practice of not cooperating with the United States, is the problem in this particular situation.[12]

Adopting the insights of Brzezinski and Symington as the basis for public policy, necessitates a change in the public *raison d'etre* for empire, the acquisition of weaponry, and the maintenance of the national apparatus. Furthermore, the old-time religion of anti-communism is not perceived as a strong enough reed to hold the interest of younger bureaucrats and military officers who quietly admire the guerrilla resistance of the Vietnamese and scorn the ideological dowdiness of the Soviet Union. The result is that a new generation of managers and bureaucrats believes that the United States has no friends or enemies—only interests. They believe that all ideals are suspect and with the blessing of the old oligarchs, look for a leader to fashion a set of ideals (outcomes) which they will pursue. This calculative understanding of the world, honed at policy sciences institutes throughout the United States, will not necessarily result in any long-term change in policy toward the Soviets. It will, however, tend to deepen the suspicion of the United States of both friendly and antagonistic nations, and this tendency will enlarge the pantheon of xenophobic fears that possess our nation from time to time. The anger of the United States has expanded to include the Arabs and Israelis while it still retains the Soviets in this pantheon. The picture is further complicated by the actions of the U.S. ambassador to the U.N., Andrew Young, who seeks to set an alternative course for U.S. policy within the U.N. and to organize support for his point of view within the government and in the society itself. He seeks to formulate a foreign policy alternative that could cause the United States to favor liberation movements. Young could end up the unwitting ally of military interventionists who will take on any cause as their own in order to justify intervention and empire.

We should not lose sight of another economic dimension to the slight shift in focus which Brzezinski predicted and which Carter's national security group seeks to bring about in international relations. Marxists economists once said that the great capitalist nations would be at loggerheads for markets for hegemonic primacy. Of course, one important purpose of an alliance system such as NATO was to avoid the Marxist taunt and prediction. However, the worldwide expansion of American corporate capitalism since the World War II and the successful economic recovery of Japan and Germany have increased the likelihood of intra-alliance conflict of the type that Brzezinski hints at and Marxists predicted. As a result, conflict between U.S. corporations and non-American corporations is of major concern to the

Carter administration. The question of whether European, U.S., and Japanese economic interests can form a system of noncompetitive, U.S.-dominated trading arrangements is at best arguable. For example, European corporations, especially French ones, are now struggling with U.S. corporations for the world's markets for products ranging from reactors to jets and missiles.

The economic power of the United States now faces several questions including whether it can invade the markets of allies and exercise dominant control without military presence; whether it can coerce alignment of multinational corporations with the social needs of the United States; whether it can invest in third world countries, thereby tying them to U.S. trading patterns; whether it can continue covert control over cabinet members of other nations without moral rebellion within the United States; and whether it can continue to play the role of world banker.

According to Robert Roosa, former undersecretary of treasury, the role of the United States as world banker is especially crucial because "we might have been forced long ago to cut down our imports (perhaps through deflation of our economy), reduce materially our foreign investments, income from which makes a substantial contribution to our current balance of payments, and curtail, perhaps sharply, our military and economic assistance to our friends and allies."[13] The balance of payments problem for the United States has become even more serious with increased sales abroad. The reason for this situation is greater alliance costs borne by the United States and multinational corporate profits which are not reinvested or taxed in the United States.

In order to retain their credibility, bankers must

give the appearance of prudence and technical competence. This is accomplished in our time by developing powerful social networks that involve private U.S. bankers in the affairs of other countries while they shape U.S. governmental policy in the economic sphere. It also requires the ideology that the dollar cannot be displaced as the international basic currency. As Carter's Undersecretary of State Richard Cooper has pointed out, there is no feasible alternative to the dollar as the world's currency, and his task is to assure the world of the power of this "truth" and the humane purpose of the great corporation.

One way some of the intellectually minded bureaucrats hope to finesse economic and military questions is through technocratic solutions in which war is declared against disease, poverty, and war itself as the instrument for imperial hegemony and stability. Economically, this is feasible for the United States because one-third of the world's trade is invoiced and transacted in dollars even though U.S. share of trade in the world market is less than one-half that amount. It is no wonder that the national security state is presently organizing the bureaucratic apparatus to take on "global systems" issues using a strong economic component. The managers of the state concern themselves in a comprehensive manner with seemingly value-neutral problems of population, scientific advances, the environment, and the elements. Kissinger presaged the positions of Carter, Brzezinski, and Vance in a speech in Los Angeles on 24 January 1975, when he said: "Progress in dealing with our traditional agenda is no longer enough . . . . The problems of energy, resources, environment, population, the uses of space and the seas, now rank with questions of military security, ideology and territorial rivalry which have traditionally made up the diplomatic agenda."[14]

Widening the consciousness of concern to include these problems as the proper national security agenda reflects several tendencies within the bureaucratic and academic community. The most significant of which is the emergence of depoliticized planning or "scanning" ideas that are meant to focus intellectual and bureaucratic institutions on particular problems which are apolitical. Examples include weather modification, ocean pollution, control of the boll weevil, the movement of plutonium from one country to another, and the control of nuclear reactors in other countries. These are seen as national security questions which can be handled only by technocrats who will dictate the political result with the aid of the police and the military. This technocratic point of view holds "that issues of global environmental and regional interdependence are not easily separable from other economic and security aspects of foreign policy. Rather these issues will be at the heart of foreign policy in coming decades, and this will have to be reflected in organizational arrangements."[15] The points made by the authors Nye, now a State Department official, and Keohane suggest the likely extension and reorganization of the national security state to include a new group of experts whose sophistication does not contradict the imperial stance. Instead, this group seeks to make the state more relevant to scientific and other questions formerly left to the civil society, to accident, or to chance.

Carter's organizational changes usher in a second and far more comprehensive stage of the national security state. In the past, the national security state was an instrument used to organize imperial stability and achieve U.S. dominance. However, its added task is the organization of nature according to bureaucratic notions of economic and technological interdependence. One example of the new tasks of the national security state is whether the United States should wage a war on the boll weevil in California and Texas. If so, how should it get the government of Mexico to do the same? Without Mexican cooperation in this war, U.S. internal efforts will accomplish little since the boll weevil will migrate south. The type of collaboration which will be sought is meant to ensure U.S. corporate and technocratic preeminence within allied states and to nurture an international leadership and mandarin class whose members will have more in common with each other than with their own societies. This cosmopolitan stance is reminiscent of the pre-twentieth century noble and kingly families that sought international family connections and identifications over national or local ones. The Trilateral Commission is both a modern and minor example of developing economic connections between the rich and the powerful across national boundaries in Western Europe, Japan, and the United States for similar purposes of control.

As the second stage of the national security state emerges more clearly, we are able to discern four tendencies that will likely conflict with each other. The first tendency is represented by Cyrus Vance. It is what some might term "soft shell" imperialism. The economic corporation is used as the instrument for U.S. hegemony on the international scene. The Vance position favors detente, believes that American technological and economic power will serve as a magnet to shape socialist and newly developing states, without having to resort to the direct use of force. Further, it can play a strong mediating role, as in the Middle East and Africa thus claiming American primacy there.

The second tendency is the emergence of technocrats who see the world as composed of a set of problems with neither enemies nor friends. They see themselves as the carriers of the scientific method, applying their skills to weather modification, adequate international food supplies and the disciplined control of modern technology. They seek the centralization of state bureaucracies, tight control over program through national budgets, and the appearance of participation and ready access to organized groups in the body politic. Such policy intellectuals see themselves as the brightest and best in a new guise. They seek to merge three modern pursuits, organization, calculation, and formation as the means of making rational judgments and controlling the future for the present social structure. They believe that technocratic solutions justify their willingness to "cede elements of national sovereignity to international entities, which alone will be able to make and monitor the necessary decisions concerning world allocation and control of populations, food, non-renewable resources, oceans and the like." [16]

The third tendency within the national security state perpetuates military growth, covert activities, preparation for war, the encouragement of modern weaponry and research, and the reluctant fulfillment of old obligations to friendly satraps. Energy advisor, James Schlesinger, Senators Moynihan of New York and Jackson of Washington, and the members of the Committee Against the Present Danger represent this point of view.

There is a fourth ambiguous tendency evidenced by

those coopted into the reorganized national security state. In the foreign affairs field, they are lonely representatives of the dreams of the 1960s. Andrew Young becomes a proponent of liberation movements calling for internal social transformation that seeks full employment, disarmament, and higher taxes for the rich and the upper middle class. Although Young appears to think otherwise, the latter set of attitudes tends to conflict with corporate and military bureaucratic needs and national technocratic attempts at colonizing the future. His civil rights experience is that the great corporations helped black people against racism. The support of the American people of these tendencies is hard to gauge. As President, Carter has acted as a vehicle for all four tendencies in proportion to their power in the society.

It is useful to remember that Carter, the engineer, came to political maturity in Georgia where there was no conflict between the small business bankers and the peanut farmers, the multinational corporations of defense (such as Lockheed), pleasure (such as Coca-Cola), and black agitation for desegregation. Indeed, in Georgia, Carter believed these forces to be quite complementary. He concluded that the task of government was to manage these forces and show their interdependence. We should not forget that Carter's ideology of leadership is based on the idea that the "Word" is more important than the social structure because it can transcend structure and institutions. We shall see whether phrases of good intention matter in the politics of bureaucratic and international conflicts. In addition, we shall also see what his word means when his choices cause backlash among those who thought his gospel was their gospel and those whom he sets out to save.

In any case, one cannot begin to understand what presidents or their advisors say without understanding the phenomenon of the national security state which changed the nature of life in the United States and the position of U.S. power and attitude in the world.

NOTES

1. By the old oligarchs, I mean nothing more than the few who think they must govern because the great wealth they own or represent is active. That is, the character of its social use and existence tends to shape the framework of the society's culture and media (the universities, schools, and museums), the national state's foreign policies (diplomatic and military policies), and the social policies of the state in their relations to the poor and middle classes. They govern for themselves and their class, and call their actions the common good.

2. Karl R. Popper, *The Spell of Plato*, vol. 1 of *The Open Society and Its Enemies*, (Princeton: Princeton University Press, 1962), p. 128.

3. Zbigniew Brzezinski, "The International Community in the Next Two Decades," in *Appendices: Commission on the Organization of Government of the Conduct of Foreign Policy*, vol. 1 (Washington: Government Printing Office, 1975), p. 17.

4. Ibid., pp. 11-19.

5. It has not escaped the attention of analysts of Eastern Europe affairs that the workers' revolt in Poland in 1970 in the coastal cities for economic demands affected the Baltic coast governmental authorities of Eastern Europe and the Soviet Union. As Charles Bettelheim has said:

> We know that they produced a profound echo among the working class of the USSR and aroused a wave of fear among the leading circles there—fear which was reflected in the revision of the economic plans for 1971, and also in intensified repression.
>
> In the USSR itself there has indeed been in recent years a tendency toward increased repression which has become more and more obvious as shown in the adoption of new police measures and in what we know of the present popu-

lation of the camps—now according to available estimates amounting to about two million. Charles Bettelheim, *Class Struggles in the USSR: First Period, 1917-1923*, trans. Brian Pearce (New York: Monthly Review Press, 1976). Originally published by Maspero/Seuil, Paris, 1974.
It is unlikely that this situation would have escaped Brzezinski's attention.

6. These include the following: NATO, the Manila Pact,. the Inter-American Treaty of Reciprocal Assistance, ANZUS, CENTO, and those with the Republic of China, the Philippines, and Pakistan.

7. Brzezinski, pp. 11-19.

8. John Connally, speech of 28 May as quoted in *U.S. News & World Report*, 14 June, pp. 52-53; quoted in Harry Magdoff and Paul M. Sweezy, *The Dynamics of American Capitalism* (New York: Monthly Review Press, 1972), p. 208.

9. The Public Agenda Foundation, *U.S. Foreign Policy: Principles for Defending the National Interest* (Washington: Carnegie Endowment for International Peace, 1976), p. 14.

10. John G. Stoessinger, "The Statesman and the Critic: Kissinger and Morgenthau," in *Truth and Tragedy: A Tribute to Hans Morgenthau*, ed. Kenneth Thompson and Robert J. Myers (New York: The New Republic Book Co., Inc., 1977), p. 228.

11. Brzezinski, p. 12.

12. Senator Stuart Symington, *Hearings on Senate Concurrent Resolution 69* U.S., Congress, Senate, Committee on Foreign Relations, (Washington: Government Printing Office, 1976), pp. 21-22.

13. Robert V. Roosa, *Monetary Reform for the World Economy*, p. 9., as quoted in Sweezy and Magdoff, *The Dynamics of American Capitalism*, pp. 230-31.

14. Henry A. Kissinger, speech of 24 January 1975 in Los Angeles, as quoted in Robert O. Keohane and J.S. Nye, "Organizing for Global Environmental and Resource Interdependence," in *Appendices: Commission on the Organization of Government for Foreign Policy*, vol. 1, p. 46.

15. Keohane and Nye, p. 48.

16. Peter Szanton, "The Future World Environment: Near-Term Problems for U.S. Foreign Policy," in *Appendices: Commission on the Organization of Government for the Conduct of Foreign Policy*, vol. 1, p. 8.

2
The Origins of the National Security State

It is impossible to understand the national security state and the reasons which give rise to the need for dismantling it without mentioning the profound and wrenching events of the last fifty years. The national security state emerges from war, from fear of revolution and change, from the economic instability of capitalism, and from nuclear weapons and military technology.[1] It has been the actualizing mechanism of ruling elites to implement their imperial schemes and misplaced ideals.[2] In practical terms, its emergence is linked to the rise of a bureaucracy that administered things and people in interchangeable fashion without concern for ends or assumptions.[3] This situation matured during a period in which the office of the president became supremely powerful as a broker and legitimating instrument of national security activity.[4]

The state system which has emerged in the United States is a constitutional deformation which menaces the freedom and well-being of its citizenry and which poses a danger to world civilization. In the last period of this century, whether the people, scholars, lawyers, judges, and members of the government can organize their understanding and their political actions so as to avert fascism or Bonapartism, a debilitating arms race that could end in the kind of horror from which there will be no redemption, and a decaying economic system which impoverishes Americans as well as people elsewhere hangs in the balance.[5]

The national security state is the means by which the dominant and achieving groups in American society organize taxation, bureaucratic, technical, and military power to support the U.S. imperial system. The ideas for structural transformation were legalized in several comprehensive pieces of legislation, the most important of which was the National Security Act of 1947. This law gave the federal government the power to mobilize and rationalize the political economy by making the military a partner in the economy. This required acceptance of the new wisdom that there were no lines between war and peace in the postwar world. The task of the National Security Council was "to advise the President with respect to the integration of domestic, foreign and military policies relating to the national security so as to enable the military services and other departments and agencies of the government to cooperate more effectively in matters involving the national security." (The term "national security" was left undefined in the act even as all manner of policy is justified in its name.)

The ideology of the national security state is tied to several geopolitical assumptions. One is that powerful military forces are necessary at all times to keep stability in a society, that no state can remain at rest and must by its nature be in constant conflict with other states preferably for "high ideals" which are taught others but not taken seriously by the leadership. This ideology also assumes that all questions of politics are questions of strategy and power, and that therefore the only issue in politics is finding the proper military and non-military instruments to obtain resources primarily for the state, in order to manifest the state's will and extend control.

While the state itself is by its nature involved in conflict with other states, its task internally is to repress, challenge or make it marginal. Its leadership is charged with the responsibility of relating social control to managing directions taken by the leadership trained or born into this "objective" way of seeing the world. The national security state is a world-wide phenomenon with client and adversary states adopting similar organizational structures.

In early 1950 through Paul Nitze and Dean Acheson, the national security state laid out its self-conscious purpose. NSC 68 was prepared. This document served as the magna carta of the national security bureaucracy. It legitimated for a generation the global conceit of the bureaucracy, opened the citizen's checkbook to the military, and adopted "strategic thinking" as the mode of governmental discourse.

In its formative stages, the organization of these efforts and their regularization was accomplished through presidential and executive order, secret memos, regulations, and bureaucratic custom (that peculiar amalgam we have described as paralaw). The transformation was justified as serving the crusade of anticommunism and the free world. In fact, the national security state superimposed itself on the nation so that the United States became less than the aggregate of its citizenry who were now to be controlled by state power. The nation (that is, its people, institutions, local cultures, its attempts at fairness, and the development of national democracy) was to be dominated and subsumed by the national security state. The national security state, composed of a conglomerate of great corporations, police and military agencies, and technical and labor elites tied their world to empire, making and preparing for war, and transforming nature into material processes for domination while parading these processes as social development. This formation process, of course, began before the World War I and developed over time.

The national security state became a means of organizing public life around massive increases in private consumption and an employment market that would be generated by direct and indirect defense and security expenditures. In political terms, the national security state concocted secrets and used oaths as mechanisms to command loyalty and respect. They operated as if these processes were the incarnation of the spirit of the American people. In reality, it represented little more than raw power leavened by bureaucratic organization. Until the movements of the 1960s, the people allowed their citizenship to atrophy and surrendered the sovereign spirit of the nation to the FBI, CIA, the Fortune 500, police organizations, and groups which had little in common with the everyday lives of the American people. Instead, these organizations and elites wrapped themselves in the flag of patriotism and molded a world historical role for their institutions using the strength and industry of the American people as the basis for their adventures.

Important organizational changes surfaced

throughout the twentieth century based on the need for a national security organization which would support imperial developments. Indeed, some U.S. government officials sought to adopt the model of the British Council of Imperial Defence. At first these recommendations were offered in such a way as to give preeminent control to Congress in matters of reorganizing the state for war preparation and mobilization. In 1911 Congressman Richmond Pearson proposed the establishment of a council of national defense which was to be dominated by the military secretaries and the six committee chairmen from Congress concerned with military affairs. The president was excluded from participation in this council because according to the Constitution, Congress has the authority to regulate the armed forces. The bill was not passed by Congress although its purposes, coordination of the military appropriations and diplomacy with economic mobilization, remain as the major goal of the national security state. The latter purpose was most clearly delineated during World War I. Many people at that time believed that the effectiveness of the U.S. government was related to the way in which the state mobilized economic resources and put down internal dissent. President Woodrow Wilson believed in the principles of strong leadership and self-determination. He took for himself war making and executive organizational functions which were previously held by Congress. Following the passage of the Overman Act in 1918, national objectives were to be defined by President Wilson, who saw no reason to include the military or the cabinet in making postwar plans. The National Defense Act of 1920 enabled the armed forces to develop the capacity for mobilization planning.

In the 1920s there was an important political debate among the ruling elites in the United States
which bore directly on this transformation process.
The bureaucratic position was reflected in the stance
taken by General Drum who argued for the creation
of a council of national defense which would act as a
military-political council. This council would develop
national mobilization plans as well as plans for the
armed forces and transportation systems. It would
have power to recommend to the president changes in
the organizational structure of the executive agencies in times of war or peace as well as expand the
federal executive agencies in time of war. Drum's
position meant a permanent transformation of the
state structure in the United States. Parenthetically,
it is important to note that General Marshall, who
was the organizational genius behind the national
security apparatus in the 1943-50 period, considered
Drum an important innovator of defense.

The second position was taken by the head of war
planning in the War Department, General Harry
Smith. General Smith's position, which prevailed
during that period, held that Drum's recommendation would cut down the military's bureaucratic au-
tonomy and that it would be better to work directly
with a president who could commandeer the economy
for the military when needed.[6] The problem with
Smith's position, according to his bureaucratic opponents, was that few believed in the military or its
solutions. This took place at the time of the Kellogg-
Briand pact which placed emphasis on negotiation
and conciliation without the use of military force or
threat. Indeed, President Hoover viewed the economic depression of the 1930s as being the result of
the rearmament of the 1920s. He had called for the

abolition of military forces to save capitalist economies. Needless to say, however, Hoover was soon drowned out by the drums of war and military Keynesianism.

In 1936 Roosevelt asked Louis Brownlow, the leading expert on administrative reorganization at the time of the New Deal, to find out whether there was legislative authority to enable him to manage the economy.[7] Brownlow told him that the World War I Council of National Defense still technically existed. This council allowed the president to comandeer the economy through an advisory committee. From 1937 on, Assistant Secretary of War Louis Johnson drew up economic and war mobilization plans which were later fashioned into an Industrial Mobilization Plan in 1939. This plan grew out of a compromise between the military and business. It was championed by such men as Karl Compton, president of MIT; Walter S. Gifford, president of American Telephone and Telegraph; Harold Moulton, president of Brookings; John Pratt, director of General Motors; and Robert Wood, president of Sears Roebuck. The plan called for the centralization of control over industrial production and mobilization. The plan would be carried out by the following four agencies: war finance, war trade, war labor, and price control. The plan foundered because labor and agriculture were not included with big business and the military. In the 1938–40 period Roosevelt was especially sensitive to charges that he was giving the economy over to the military and big business through the War Resources Board. The fear of business was that the military would take over preeminent control of the economy under the guise of military preparedness and never give it back. From 1931 onward the various military services had put forward plans for defense which would have put the services in a preeminent position. The history of the Bureau of the Budget during World War II notes that General Brehon Somervell, chief of Army Service Forces, "prepared a plan in May of 1942 that would have put the War Production Board and the economy under the newly created Joint Chiefs of Staff."[8] This plan was rejected by the president.

As Lieutenant General William Y. Smith has pointed out in an extraordinarily interesting thesis, the struggle for control over the economic and industrial mobilization between the civilians and the military was not resolved during the war. "The military departments constantly pressured the President for more control over the war economy. He met their demands by insuring them important positions in mobilization agencies."[9]

In 1945 the United States emerged from the Second World War as the most powerful nation in the world. Its allies were dependent on the United States for economic aid to restore the social and economic structures of the prewar period. The vanquished were, of course, totally dependent on the largesse of the United States. It was no wonder that U.S. leaders felt a certain omnipotence and hubris during the immediate postwar period. The new power of the United States could not be denied. U.S. technology, with help from European scientists, had scaled the heights to become the destroyer of worlds with the invention of the atomic bomb.

American leaders attempted to define for the world the meaning of democracy and freedom. They seemed to have earned that right. Needless to say, if its purpose were symmetric justice, there was ironies in this enterprise. While the United States blocked the

Soviets' attempt to get $10 billion in heavy machinery reparations from the German Ruhr on the grounds that the Germans had suffered enough, the U.S. government had little interest in aiding 110,000 illegally incarcerated Japanese-Americans in California in their attempt to regain their property at the end of the war.

Yet even in the context of omnipotence, there remained a profound doubt about the strength of the economic and political systems of the United States. The year 1945 came only a few years after the bread lines of the depression and the time of a broken-spirited people who believed that something was wrong with them because they could not find work. After the war, this doubt was fueled by strikes in all major industries. Most unions had accepted a no-strike pledge during the Second World War in exchange for certain minor management perogatives. However, these arrangements were dissolved at the end of the war when Truman threatened to take over the coal mines and railroads. Economists predicted but were partially wrong that the American economy would plunge back into its pre-World War II torpor.

Thus, American leadership and the society itself, faced an important contradiction. On the one hand, the United States as a nation had gained enormous prestige and material power from World War II. It was honored and respected by communists and colonized people alike. Indeed, the Communist Party in the United States under Earl Browder dissolved itself and became an association. According to him, the capitalists in the United States were different from the European brand who had no progressive aspects. Like the American people, he believed their capitalists were not class bound. Revolutionaries like

Ho Chi Minh sought aid from the United States in modeling their Constitution and Declaration of Independence after the eighteenth century documents of the United States. Businessmen who feared the New Deal admitted to its political success when it was identified with Franklin Roosevelt's war policies.

On the other hand, New Deal and Truman planners knew that the Roosevelt effort to build a stable social democracy failed prior to the war. The New Deal, as the gifted social historian Geoffrey Perrett said, offered a hope. It was hardly able to institute accomplishments which other nations in Western Europe had adopted more than a generation earlier. For example, Roosevelt was fearful of putting forward a national health insurance program for fear that Congress would vote down the entire Social Security Act.

As Perrett pointed out, the Second World War was a collective social experience which brought access to higher education for millions of people, a modern civil rights movement, emphasis on finding a democratic purpose to the nation, and redistribution of national income.[10] It was just this set of forces and programs which emerged from the Second World War that had to be limited because their tidal wave proportions could also have resulted in a progressive formation that would have altered the economic system moving it toward democratic reconstruction. This consideration must be kept in mind when thinking about the economic role of the national security state.

The national security state apparatus was fashioned from the organizational shells and technological feats of the Second World War. Liberals saw this apparatus as a way to maintain civilian control. For example, the Atomic Energy Commission and the Atomic Energy Act were both parts of national security state legislation. The Atomic Energy Act was hailed by civil libertarians, scientists, and the press for retaining civilian control of atomic bombs. In reality, the victory was a pyrrhic one. Differences of policy between the AEC and the military were of the most minor nature; this should have been recognized by scientists at the time the bill became law. James R. Newman the liberal whose name was to be sent to the Senate for approval as an atomic energy commissioner, was withdrawn by Truman because Newman was thought to be friendly with antimilitary scientists. To liberals, the CIA was a means of overcoming the State Department's narrow mode of political and diplomatic reporting. Liberals explained that the Departments of War and Navy had to be replaced with the Department of Defense due to the new role of the United States in the world.

Holding back the excesses of Congress and the Right on the issue of communists and the Left was also viewed as a liberal victory; to this end, President Truman set up the Loyalty and Security Board. In 1950 Hubert Humphrey insisted on the passage of the Communist Control Act so that liberals would appear to be as loyal as were the conservatives. Piece by piece, each executive order and law served as a significant building block in the structure of the national security state. Later Truman would claim that the National Security Act of 1947 did not countenance the CIA becoming a rogue elephant. Nevertheless, he was aware of covert uses in which the CIA was put to in Europe and Asia. And all presidents since the Second World War have been fascinated by the dual life of the covert agent. As one astute commentator has said, "Because covert operations have an intrinsic appeal to the activist, manipulative personality types who are attracted to centers of power, the United States and other powers, will retain at least a standby capability in this area."[11]

Even the Marshall Plan, postwar government planning at its most generous, was organized by the manipulative personality types. Its leading planner was Richard Bissell who became the deputy director of plans (covert operations) for the CIA in 1950. Incidentally, ten years later, in 1960-61, he planned the Bay of Pigs adventure. Over 90 percent of the 14 billion dollars given to Western Europe under the Marshall Plan was spent in the United States. It was an important tool used to stabilize the economic system at home once pent-up demand was met after the Second World War. According to Kolko and Solberg, with the exception of Germany, Europe had already recovered when the United States initiated the Marshall Plan. On the other hand, the plan was helpful in subsidizing U.S. enterprises. For example, it stimulated the growth of the entire cotton industry. Will Clayton, undersecretary of state and the leading cotton broker in the United States, developed the Marshall Plan with an eye to increasing cotton exports. The southern chairmen of congressional committees on foreign relations, appropriations, and armed services were, of course, pleased with this subtle way of financing U.S. industry and agriculture. This form of financing turned out to be costly for blacks because the subsequent large orders from Europe placed in the 1948-50 period encouraged the plantation owners to mechanize. The result was a surplus in the labor force which resulted in the continual migration of blacks to northern cities after the Second World War.

A remarkably clever and successful agricultural program geared to the internal dynamics of the U.S. economy but with profound effect on beneficiary nations was the Food for Peace Act (P.L. 480). It was aimed at guaranteeing old markets for U.S. agricultural products while expanding into new markets. It provided cash to farmers without the need for the United States to store the produce in this country. P.L. 480 also became an important tool used by the United States in directing weak economies. The recipient country buys the U.S. farm surplus with its currency. The currency, however, stays in the recipient country in accounts controlled by the United States. These accounts are often used to buy military equipment or pay U.S. obligations overseas.[12]

Domestically, the national security state operated as a stabilizing mechanism and legitimated intervention in the economy through defense procurement. A rather large part of the economy was stabilized and within certain parameters corporations such as General Electric that dealt with the government were protected against loss or economic collapse.[13] Government economists and Congress believed that if such corporations could be protected there would be a positive multiplier effect in other parts of the economy. Military production and facilities were used to develop the United States. This had a positive economic consequence on the housing market and resulted in comprehensive highway construction. Accordingly, defense installations including missile plants and arsenals often were built to create a wholesome effect on local business and employment conditions. It was the political task of the congressman to get the Defense Department to install military facilities in their respective congressional districts. The seniority system in Congress, which favors one-party states, enabled the South to take the greatest advantage of this method of economic subsidization where wages and prices have been significantly lower than other regions of the United States.

At the end of World War II, economists believed there would be a permanent 8-10 percent unemployment rate following military demobilization. They did not anticipate the pent-up demands and personal cash reserves which would be unleased once wartime limits on buying were lifted. They also failed to consider corporate planning which was remarkably successful as a planning device. Gardiner Means, the executive director of the Committee for Economic Development, undertook an important empirical study which produced creative results. The CED asked leading corporate heads how much they would produce at the end of World War II. They then told likely suppliers and producers what to expect from fellow corporate leaders. The CED served as a coordinating instrument of demobilization. Its practical role was that of an information broker helping to reestablish a market. They predicted that there would be no depression and used their own work to ensure that result.

New Deal planners began a postwar committee which outlined and later developed the G.I. Bill. This revivified the universities and simultaneously transformed them into government instruments for transferring income. The G.I. Bill, of course, also operated as a social security program by taking men off the labor market. In addition, it reinforced the self-fulfilling modern illusion that academic education is an important prerequisite to employment.

The military demobilization process was politically important for the reason that soldiers attempted to leave the armed forces, riots occurred at American military bases across the world, and parents demanded that their young men aged eighteen to twenty be sent home. There was a smell of popular discontent among the troops. In many cases, the U.S. soldiers favored resistance groups which included or were led by socialists and communists. The *New York Times* pointed out that the marines in China privately sympathized with the communists in 1946 although the orders of the leaders were, of course, to protect the nationalist troops and regime.[14]

While most soldiers and sailors wanted to get out of the armed forces as quickly as possible, military and civilian leaders had other ideas. They sought a system of universal military training, and they sought to secure a world-wide empire which seemed to grow naturally out of the Second World War. The international context was turbulent and lent itself to great power paternalism as old empires were dying. The Dutch were losing their foothold in Indonesia, the French colonials were beginning their military struggle to reassert control over the Vietnamese people in 1945, and the English disgorged control over India. The Japanese withdrew from China, Korea, and various islands in the Pacific, and German forces were beaten in Western and Eastern Europe thus surrendering their imperial domain. The diplomats invoked eighteenth century phrases from physics, such as "power vacuum" to suggest that the United States had to fill the vacuum before someone else did. For example, why shouldn't the United States continue its military intervention in China? It had 53,000 marines in Northern China and Manchuria.

The United States was also giving great amounts of lend-lease to the Chinese nationalist armed forces, and it was moving the nationalist troops around Northern China so that Chiang could control the transportation and communications lines there.

Since this was the period of decolonization, a series of incidents was read by leaders in the United States as either examples of new power vacuums left behind by the declining European empires (vacuums which had to be filled by the United States) or as opportunities for U.S. influence to keep the Soviet Union in check as a second class power and to consolidate its global hegemonic position. Each judgment, if contradicted, was viewed as a *casus belli* by high U.S. officials. Nevertheless, from 1945 to 1948, the leadership was faced with the conflict between the average American's desire to get out of war, the elite's desire to set up an empire on a rational basis, and the desires of certain influential organizations who pressed preventive war strategies to secure the century of the United States.

The national security state itself was an instrumental means in preparing for war but not for having continuous war. The United States was to be perpetually engaged and armed accordingly, but the United States was not to engage in a world war with the Soviet Union. Men like George Kennan, the architect of the containment policy, hoped that their policy papers on the Soviet Union would strengthen those bureaucratic forces within the Truman administration which did not want to have a preventive war against the Soviet Union. It should be remembered that even humanist liberal thinkers like Bertrand Russell were counseling preventive nuclear war with the Soviet Union while the United States and Great

Britain held the monopoly on nuclear weapons. Within the United States, the jingoist move for preventive war to establish the century of the United States, and Senator Robert Taft's antimilitary isolationism, could only be defeated if a consensus developed around the principles of internal stability, anti-communism, and a commitment to world hegemony without major war. This required a purge of the Left in the United States in both major institutions and the government and isolating Taft's fear of imperial involvement as patently wrong-headed.

By the beginning of the Korean War, leftist liberals and the Left in the United States found themselves the object of great harassment. With the crushing defeat of Henry Wallace in 1948, the Left was eliminated from policy debates on the character of legislation for social welfare and the international stance of the United States. (As we shall see, the nature of the debate took on new and surprising forms in the 1960s which were not contemplated by the national security state and its apparatus.) The effect of the Truman loyalty probe and those later undertaken by Senator Joseph McCarthy of Wisconsin, Pennsylvania Congressman "Tam" Walter, and J. Edgar Hoover was to enforce a world view based on an automatic defense of corporate capitalism as the reason for prosperity in the United States and justification of covert and overt military adventures and alliances. The FBI and other police agencies of the federal government proceeded to set the standards for what was permissible and what was impermissible in politics and dissent in the United States. Many who held positions in such institutions as labor unions, the media, and universities were purged. Liberals, including the ACLU, rallied around Hoover saying that he was a professional and

that communist hunting should be left to the professionals in the FBI. Some liberals knew better, but
this point of view was manufactured as a position of
lesser evil. It was meant to forestall other parts of the
Right, the American Legion, and Congress from taking the lead in carrying out purges. Workers on government contracts were and still are required to sign
loyalty oaths to the national security system. Workers and scientists learned that there were secrets that
could be kept from them, even though it was they who
had created the contents of the secret. Of course, the
way in which a secret is defined and the person who
defines it were not open to debate among the
citizenry. The secrecy and purge system helped the
national security state to internalize the assumptions of capitalism as a world system and "the free
world," and allowed the use of military power for its
worldwide growth.

For the first time in the history of the United
States, there was a strong belief among U.S. leaders
that class conflict could be muted, managed, and
perhaps transcended. The trade union movement lost
interest in building an independent left or socialist
alternative. The dream of increasing the economic
pie had taken hold. It was filled with the cream of
consumer goods and topped with the slightly bitter
cherry of economic growth. Expansion masked the
question of who would cut the share and what the
shares meant in terms of quality of life and social
services. As part of the consensus process, the two
parties forged a coalition around national security
policy which included both foreign and domestic aspects. The doubters of the Right, Taft and Bender
among others, believed that the thrust toward military empire and entangling alliances would destroy

free enterprise at home and sharply curtail the influence of Congress in foreign and national security affairs. But their voices were drowned on the Senate floor by their fellow Republicans. The Eightieth Republican-dominated Congress favored the development of the national security state and joined Truman and the executive branch composed of such men as Tom Clark, James Byrnes, the military chiefs, in fashioning the contours of the postwar state enterprise. They agreed that politics stops at the water's edge. John McCloy, an adviser to presidents and bank presidents, once said that the difference between the Republican and Democratic parties was in whether the trustees or the professors of the universities would advise the state. The advice, McCloy believed, would be the same in all essential aspects.[15] For nearly twenty years, it was assumed that the disagreements in public policy did not concern ends but means. Liberal ideologists, such as Arthur Schlesinger, referred to a "vital center" which legitimated the narrowness of debate. It was the task of liberals to screen out views as well as people that did not fit into the consensus.

The most powerful intellectual exponent of the national security state and the cold war was the theologian Reinhold Niebuhr. He argued that internally the United States had reached a partnership between capital and labor and that this partnership could be maintained if organized labor were given a role in the national security system. Politically, Niebuhr's ideas fit well with a time that wanted to mask its oligarchy with mass democracy. Although it was not Niebuhr's belief, the national security state retained the assumption that the quantum of knowledge and the spirit of the society rest with the rich, the well born and those among the bright who seek a place with the rich and well born.[16]

Internationally, Niebuhr argued that the struggle in the world was between the forces of light and of darkness. He further argued that the United States as a state could not be expected to act morally. Because Niebuhr was an activist who served as chairman of the advisory committee of the State Department's policy planning staff in 1947 and an influential writer in scholarly and current journals, his views strongly influenced the course of the cold war. They also rationalized the development of the CIA, the dirty tricks, and the covert operations which allowed for massive intervention abroad. Furthermore, Niebuhr justified the buildup of nuclear weapons without concern for the decaying moral effects such weaponry had on the society. As George Kennan once said, "He was the father of us all."[17]

The owners of the mass media also joined in the crusade. They saw their role in encouraging covert schemes of propaganda and espionage as the way to win the cold war. The chairman of the board of RCA, General David Sarnoff, called for training underground resistance movements in "satellite nations, and China and Russia proper . . . to provide leadership for resistance operations; to engage in propaganda, subversion, infiltration of the enemy; even to carry on administrative and civic work *after* the collapse of the Communist regimes" [Sarnoff's italics].[18] The major media, including the *New York Times*, NBC, and the now defunct *New York Herald Tribune*, were used as covers for the sorts of activities Sarnoff described.

The patriotic excesses of General Sarnoff were tempered by Dwight Eisenhower during his presidency. Eisenhower was the most successful leader of the national security state. He understood the state's limits and the destabilizing effects of war; he also understood that the military itself could be kept in line and be controlled by a balanced budget and a limited defense budget. He accomplished an impressive achievement in bringing the defense budget from 89 billion down to 40 billion dollars within six years. Ike also insisted that the military take an oath of allegiance to the business system. Maxwell Taylor, in *The Uncertain Trumpet*, describes a scene in which he is expected to heel to civilian control. In practical terms, this meant subservience to the business community as symbolized by men like Secretary of Defense Wilson of GM and Treasury Secretary Humphrey of Mark Hanna Mining.[19]

Liberals complained that his terms were marked with two recessions. Of course, Eisenhower was not the spokesman for Norman Thomas and the Socialist Party or, for that matter, the social democratic ADA which favored big defense budgets and social welfare programs. Full employment was not his concern nor was it that of the business class. He and the Republicans were prepared to accept and indeed courted unemployment because fewer workers, high productivity, and tax breaks to change costly machinery were the means of securing high corporate profits. Eisenhower's real success, however, was in the area of national security because he was able to control the military.

He and Dulles concluded a number of pacts (SEATO, ANZUS, and Baghdad) interpreted as military assistance while shying away from direct military engagement. As part of this strategy, Eisenhower built up U.S. paramilitary covert operations and encouraged the covert apparatus in Southeast Asia. In addition, he and the Dulles brothers together with William Donovan, who had been the head of the OSS during the Second World War and later became ambassador to Thailand in 1953, set the pattern of limited involvement through the CIA satrap system. When Allen Dulles became the head of the CIA, General Bedell Smith (the former director of the CIA) became undersecretary of state and thus the deputy to John Foster Dulles. Such moves are more than casual or playful changes on the part of leaders. In this case, they were meant to integrate the covert and intelligence operations apparatus with the creation of worldwide diplomatic hegemony without war.

Eisenhower had learned that the Korean War was a costly enterprise and U.S. generals such as Matthew Ridgeway were utterly opposed to any military reengagement of U.S. troops for war in Asia. The high costs of the Korean War required informal, less onerous means of operating the empire than that requiring direct military intervention by U.S. forces. In 1954 Dien Bien Phu proved to be the moment of testing a less costly strategy than limited war. Dulles appeared to champion the use of nuclear weapons in Indochina. He and Nixon wanted to give two or three nuclear weapons to France or stage a U.S. raid, to be called Operation Vulture, in Indochina. Eisenhower, a clever bureaucratic fox, said that before the United States could give the nuclear weapons, Dulles would have to obtain the support of the leaders of Congress and of the allies of the United States. Needless to say, no support was found, and Admiral Radford's military strategy went untested.[20]

At the end of his first term, Eisenhower stopped the

French, British, and Israelis from destroying Egypt's nascent power in the Middle East. Eisenhower served notice on U.S. allies that only the United States could take independent action in the world. Other allies would have to seek permission if they wanted to be supported by the United States. The Hungarian revolt against the Soviet occupation occurred at the same time as the invasion of Egypt. Many people in the United States were emboldened and saw this revolt as the chance of a rollback in Eastern Europe. Eisenhower, however, refused to entertain any thoughts of direct military intervention even though the CIA had been directly involved in adding fuel to the anticommunist, anti-Soviet fire in Hungary. The postwar line of circa 1947 was fixed and U.S. national concerns included modest interest in Eastern Europe except for the use of symbolic propaganda and mischief-making. One such example of interest occurred from 1947 to 1974 when Cardinal Mindzenty, a target of the Communist Party in Hungary, was sheltered in the U.S. embassy.

Dulles, Acheson, and others feared any diplomatic move that might shake the status quo in Europe even though Dulles campaigned for the Republican Party and espoused the forward strategy of rollback and liberation. When faced with the possibility of just such a rollback, however, Dulles was not interested.

Rollback has come in various forms. During the latter 1950s, European nations, including Poland and the Soviet Union, put forth a variety of disengagement plans. The interest of Poland was to allow itself a breath of freedom as its plan called for removing Soviet troops from various places in Eastern Euorope including Poland. The Soviets supported the Rapacki disengagement plan as a means of stopping the rearming of Germany and shaking the NATO alliance which it saw as a threat to itself. Some Americans such as Senator Hubert Humphrey and George Kennan believed in disengagement because they saw it as an alternative way of penetrating Eastern Europe. It was a subtle rollback policy against the Soviet Union.

Eisenhower emotionally favored a cutback. He feared, however, that the entire national security state system would unravel. He would then be faced with charges of being soft on communism, of destroying the U.S. base in Europe, and of encouraging the heresy of neutralism. After all, Eisenhower had arranged for the neutralization of Austria, and it would have appeared that the entire cold war was about to be liquidated. The Republicans, among themselves, together with the Democratic Party feared a McCarthyist attack. McCarthyism scared the national security agencies as well as Eisenhower because of its unpredictability and irrationality. They believed that McCarthyism represented populism and the Irish sections of the American Catholic Church which could be used as a weapon against the elements critical to imperial thrust including established power, the prestige of universities, and the military system.

From 1955 to 1960 when disengagement plans were seriously discussed, there was a significant chance of disarmament. It was, however, sacrificed by Eisenhower at the insistence, indeed connivance, of Dulles. Harold Stassen, Eisenhower's advisor on disarmament, worked with the Soviet envoy Zorin to limit missiles, bombers, and troops in Europe. The agreement was initialed by both Zorin and Stassen. Dulles and the U.S. military were frightened by this change in U.S.-Soviet relations. Dulles relieved Stassen as head of the delegation and personally took charge. He added more conditions to the agreement. The Soviets backed out, and the single most important chance for disarmament ended. This failure destroyed the chance for Soviet disengagement in Eastern Europe.

There were structural reasons for Dulles' action. The U.S. military was at a technological turning point in that it was about to enter the missile age. Needless to say, any diplomatic negotiation attempting to settle differences might cause a slowdown in the arms race and thereby lose the strength and influence of the national security corporations and military. It is interesting to note that Kissinger, in order to get some measure of detente with the Soviet Union, agreed to keep the arms race going through SALT and therefore preserve the power as well as allegiance of the various national security corporations.

During this period, the Democratic Party, Nelson Rockefeller, and much of the Wall Street establishment were enamoured of the arms race and the new arms technology. The Rockefellers had large investments in missiles and nuclear power. Liberals insisted on high military budgets and greater expenditures for research and development. Manufacturers and financiers (partly for investment reasons), the military (because it sought a first strike capability, that is, a successful preventive war capability), and the scientists (because they enjoyed their new-found potency) all pressed Eisenhower on the so-called missile gap. The gap, as a matter of fact, did exist, but it was the Soviets who were behind. This fear became the great theme of the presidential race in 1960. The Democratic Party's themes in the campaign were based on the policy conclusions of the Rockefeller brothers panels and the Gaither Commission Report which called for substantial increases in missiles, in tactical and limited war capability, as well as in civil defense. While Eisenhower had not been able to bring about arms control and disarmament, he was at least successful in holding back some of the more frightening forces and recommendations until the Democratic Party returned to power.

One such recommendation was propounded by Maxwell Taylor. He assumed that the nuclear deterrent was not credible in confronting revolutionary war or wars of national liberation. He proposed that the army adopt the strategy of flexible response and therefore the ideology of direct military intervention where necessary. The flexible response would put teeth into the various pacts which Dulles had drawn. Eisenhower rejected the brush fire war strategy as one which would involve great costs and risks for the United States, but Taylor's strategy was adopted by President Kennedy. In addition, Maxwell Taylor became Kennedy's military advisor and chairman of the Joint Chiefs of Staff. Taylor hoped to develop the type of overwhelming U.S. military forces which would presumptively destroy guerrilla or liberation movements quickly and completely. But police actions of imperial powers are hard to implement, as Taylor found out when he was sent as ambassador to Vietnam by Johnson.[21] Indeed, neither Taylor, the French General Navarre, nor Westmoreland was a match for Giap's concept of the people's war.

Eisenhower appeared to understand that there are two purposes for armaments monopoly by states. One purpose is to control activity internally in such a way as to keep the structure of power exactly as it is. This practice is true in both socialist and capitalist countries. Thus, the police, armed forces, and the internal police systems exist to support their own bureaucratic power and the current ideological system of which they are a part. Consequently, a new disarmament strategy should take into account the internally repressive role of armaments, their relationship to the international arms race, and the fact that the arms race is an independent factor which justifies the existence, power, and status of national bureaucratic institutions in the public and private sectors.

The second purpose for state armaments is as an instrument to intimidate, persuade, or fight other nations. This is ordinarily thought of as the arms system, but both systems are interdependent. Thus, the international system of the arms race with its attendant scientists, military, and producers of raw materials supports the ongoing internal power structure of nation-states. Paradoxically, the period of detente between the United States and the Soviet Union seems to have had an invigorating effect on the arms race. The race to cataclysm has intensified as the bureaucratic institutions of the Soviet Union and the United States organize their technical, strategic, and bureaucratic ideologies along similar and correlative lines.

NOTES

1. See generally R. Barnet, *Intervention and Revolution: The United States in the Third World* (1968); L.B. Johnson, *The Vantage Point* (1971); J. O'Connor, *The Fiscal Crisis of the State* (1973); Marcus Raskin, *Being and Doing* (1971); R. Stavins, R. Barnet, and M. Raskin, *Washington Plans an Aggressive War* (1971); R. Borosage, "The Making of the National Security State," in *The Pentagon Watchers: Student Report on the Na-*

tional Security State, ed. L. Rodberg and D. Shearer, 1970; Marcus Raskin, "The Kennedy Hawks Assume Power from the Eisenhower Vultures", in *The Pentagon Watchers: Student Report on the National Security State*.

2. C. Wright Mills, *The Power Elite* (1956), pp. 274-78.

3. Marcus Raskin, "The Megadeath Intellectuals", *New York Review of Books*, 14 November 1963.

4. G. Novack, *Democracy and Revolution* (1971); Marcus Raskin, *Notes on the Old System* (1974).

5. Marcus Raskin, *The Common Good* (New York, Simon & Schuster, to be published in 1979).

6. Lt. General William Y. Smith, "The Search for National Security Planning Machinery," (Ph.D. diss., Harvard University, 1960), pp. 177-86.

7. Ibid., p. 225; see also *U.S. Presidential Committee on Administration Management in the Government of the United States* (Washington: Government Printing Office, 1937), p. 3.

8. W. Smith, p. 341; compare with Civilian Production Administration, *Industrial Mobilization for War* (Washington: Government Printing Office, 1947), p. 979.

9. W. Smith, p. 319.

10. Geoffrey Perrett, *Days of Sadness, Years of Triumph: The American People, 1939-1945* (Baltimore, Md.: Penguin Books, Inc., 1973), p. 11, also see pp. 441-43.

11. Paul W. Blackstock, "Intelligence, Covert Operations, and Foreign Policy," in *Appendices: Commission on the Organization of Government for Foreign Policy* vol. 7, p. 101.

12. James Warner Bjorkman, "Public Law 480 and the Policies of Self-Help and Short-Tether: Indo-American Relations, 1965-68," in *Appendices: Commission on the Organization of Government for Foreign Policy*, vol. 7, pp. 192-209.

13. General Electric designed and built nuclear reactors, a financial loser, at the urging of the Atomic Energy Commission.

14. John Gittings, *The World and China, 1922-1972* (New York: Harper and Row, Publishers, 1974), p. 121; *New York Times* article appeared 19 August 1946.

15. John J. McCloy, speech of 14 April 1961 on disarmament, U.S. Department of State publication.

16. The spirit used to be the province of the upper classes. Before the upper classes, the spiritual idea which acted as the instrument of political legitimation in societies was controlled by

the king who received this gift from God. When the divine right was received from God it meant, by religious definition, that the king was able to do anything necessary in the name of God, who obviously could not be immoral. But this view of divine right and political power did change. Once people believed that divine right should be reposed in the community as a whole, it was clear that good and evil needed a common or community definition. However, theory did not meet practice. The state required that an elite should govern and define good and evil.

17. Reinhold Niebuhr, *The Children of Light and the Children of Darkness* (New York: 1950); Arthur Schlesinger's review of Niebuhr's *Irony of American History* in *Christianity and Society*, 17 (1952): pp. 25-27; both are noted in Morton White, "Epilogue for 1957" in *Social Thought in America: The Revolt Against Formalism* (New York: Oxford University Press, 1949), pp. 247-80; Kennan quote is noted by Carl Solberg in *Riding High* (New York: Mason and Lipscomb Publishers, 1973), pp. 47-49.

18. Hahn and Neff, eds., *American Strategy for the Nuclear Age* (New York: Doubleday-Anchor Publishers, 1960), pp. 426, 436.

19. Maxwell Taylor, *The Uncertain Trumpet* (New York: Harper and Row, 1960), pp. 115-29.

20. Chalmers M. Roberts, "The Day We Didn't Go to War," in *The Vietnam Reader*, ed. Marcus Raskin and Bernard B. Fall (New York: Random House, 1965), pp. 57-66.

21. Taylor, *The Uncertain Trumpet*; Marcus G. Raskin, "The Kennedy Hawks Assume Power from the Eisenhower Vultures," in *The Pentagon Watchers: Students Report on the National Security State*, ed. Leonard S. Rodberg and Derek Shearer (Garden City, N.Y.: Doubleday and Co., Inc. 1970), pp. 65-98, especially pp. 89-90.

3
Working People and the National Security State

The policy decisions of business, government elites, and unions at the end of the Second World War were to a large extent shaped by the crisis of employment and work. The Employment Act of 1946 laid the basis for relative labor peace within the United States. While it was not a full employment act, it had the effect of supporting the contention that capitalism was being tamed, and that workers had a stake in the maintenance of capitalism. The act acknowledged the role of the federal government in finding ways to help workers cushion themselves in an oligopoly economy. It became an important peg in the national security state because it isolated the organized from the unorganized. It, thus, placed an iron curtain between those workers who received benefits from their unions and those workers who were mostly unorganized and received no benefits from the state or through union contracts. Since the end of World War II, fewer than 25 percent of American workers have been organized into trade unions.[1]

The power of the labor movement was carefully circumscribed. Passed over the veto of Truman in

June 1947, the Taft-Hartley Act made clear that labor unions were merely junior partners in the political economy. As the lawyer of the AFL-CIO, and former Justice Arthur Goldberg said, the act had been "used to block union organization, to weaken unions and to interfere with free collective bargaining."[2] At the time the Taft-Hartley Act was passed, two-thirds of American workers were employed in open shops.[3]

The national security state was successful in maintaining a labor movement without a leftist consciousness. In the mid-1940s management feared that a socialist direction would destroy the whole corporate structure. Corporate and military leaders found themselves in a paradoxical situation during the Second World War. They were caught in war production which by its nature is socialized. They feared that the socialized productive process would result in socialized control. In order, to forestall a socialist impulse, it was necessary to integrate the labor movement into the national security state and allow management to take full control over the assembly line. This was accomplished through several methods after the Second World War. One method was the dismantling of the War Production Board which included union leaders as members. During the war, this public body comprised of union and management members helped to enforce production goals and coparticipated in controlling the life of the plant. Certain important gains were won which set a pattern for defining worker decency. For example, the board established the right, if not the reality, of women workers to receive "equal work for equal pay."[4]

The net effect of the abolition of the War Production Board was to limit union demands to wage benefits. As the reader knows, the fact that the issue between management and labor was reduced in scope to one of wage benefits did not mean that such benefits were granted without very difficult and costly strikes. During the Second World War, stoppages were kept to a minimum through grievance procedures worked out by the board. Unions took a no-strike pledge which labor leaders championed including those ostensibly involved with the Communist Party. The no-strike pledge increased wild cat work stoppages since during the war period wages increased by only 15 percent while the cost of living increased by 45 percent. Labor union leaders at the end of the war were emboldened by the statistic that "in the six prewar years, 1934-39, they [the corporations] had aggregated 26 billion dollars. But between 1940 and 1945, the war period, profits amounted to 117 billion—four and a half times what corporations reported in net profit during the preceding six years."[5]

A series of successful strikes were called in the steel, auto, and electric industries at the end of the war which gained workers about an eighteen cents an hour increase in their pay. The labor movement as a whole, however, backed away from the strike-to-work move at Brewster Aviation in 1944 where 4000 workers seized the factory when faced with being laid off. Although union strategists and leaders did not support sit downs and other tactics which would have changed the real property relations between workers and corporations, owners and managers greatly feared the power of a mass labor movement which was less than ten years old. It was thought that this movement might successfully eliminate the open shop and thereby begin a *de facto* change in the nature of management perogatives. The economic bill of rights proposed by Roosevelt in his final state of the union address seemed to give the blessings of the federal government to increased labor union activity concerning the issue of the right to a job and a decent living. Roosevelt's death and the election of the Republican-dominated eightieth Congress which fought the Left and the communists at home and abroad reenforced the swing to conservatism and a strong antilabor attitude through legislation and hearings of intimidation.

The arrangements worked out in the early postwar period are to no little extent responsible for the present character of income and wealth distribution in the United States. As Lester Thurow of MIT pointed out, distribution patterns in the United States are very similar to those that are found in the poorest and most reactionary nations—nations in which the U.S. national security managers seek reforms because they are so outrageous and politically unstable.[6]

The Taft-Hartley Act was an important peg in sustaining maldistribution. The most important objective was to halt the organization of the labor movement. It also included a weakening of the shop steward system so that workers could take their grievances directly to employers without benefit of the union mechanism. It encouraged separate unions organized around skills so that crafts people would not organize with unskilled workers. The most important aspect of the Taft-Hartley Act, from the standpoint of national security, was to exclude any whose officers refused to take a noncommunist oath from the National Labor Relations Board. Thus, workers could not choose leadership that might in any way shake the national security hegemony of that time. Congressional committees would investigate union officers for charges of communism or perjury at the time of union elections in order to vote in the officially sanctioned group. Autonomous politics stopped inside the workplace and in international affairs and was replaced by the cold war consciousness of manipulated assent and dissent.

After the political demise of Henry Wallace in 1948 and the passage of the Taft-Hartley Act, the working class learned that it no longer had its own purpose or consciousness. As a result of the Second World War and its positive effect on consumer goods distribution, laborers were told that they had become members of the middle class. But this curious middle class had no real property that would provide it with investment discretion or independence of thought and action. There was a shift in legal categories as well. The various acts concerning labor arrangements relations and the Employment Act of 1946 changed workers into employees. If I am employed by you, I am either to do work for you, or perform a service for you. I do not have a consciousness which is independent of you. Thus, employment is an extension of the feudal and then common law concept of master-servant relationships. The subtle use of status language continues even today. Unions call for full employment instead of saying that every person is a worker and does productive work and is therefore entitled to full rights. The members of the working class considered themselves as employees and were so described in labor legislation. As long as we continue to describe work in terms of employment, we perpetuate status relationships.

The employment characterization is an important

peg in the cold war as workers are tied to the products made by their employers. For example, the progressive United Auto Workers is not only the union of the auto workers, it is also the union of workers in the aerospace industry. The oil workers' union also includes atomic energy workers. Discovering ways in which unions can help workers escape the cold war when their jobs and the power of a particular union are tied to war production and the number of its members, remains a critical problem for labor leaders and workers who are antiimperial and peace-oriented.

The new middle class which once had independence, property, and skill now had leisure goods and consumption patterns. This change in the definition of the middle class had its origins in the New Deal. Marriner Eccles, chairman of the Federal Reserve Board, held the view that consuming power should not be allowed to lag and public works programs were necessary to keep consumption going; if high consumption were interrupted, capitalism would collapse.[7] Accordingly, the working class was transformed into the middle class through the process of consumer advertising and easy credit for consumer goods.

Americans were encouraged through advertising to crave consumer goods. They produced and were provided an infinite variety of them. It appeared that consumers had many choices. Freedom and democracy came to be understood as consumer choice. The acquisition of consumer goods was the way American families showed others that they were part of the middle class society. It was taken for granted that fulfillment which could not be found in work could come through leisure. Television played an extraordinarily important role in the hustling of dreams and consumer goods and the apparent leveling up of all groups to societal norms. The media created the illusion (to some extent true, in practice) that everybody used the same soap and cared about cleanliness, everybody wore the same clothes, and everybody drove the same cars.

Product acquisition and consumption were critical for one's sexuality and feelings of potency. Cars became a material necessity as more people lived far from their places of work and there was no form of socially-owned or devised alternative transportation. Yet politicians geared their thoughts to mass problems in a crude, undifferentiated way wherein everyone was engaged in the same dream and worry. President Johnson once said that Americans were worried about two things: the men were worried about whether they could "get it up" and the women were worried about "cancer of the titty."

The modern corporate ideology, with its emphasis on selling leisure and consumer goods and translating all services into a money-price system, has had a destructive effect on both work as creative activity and the work ethic itself. As Ralph Borsodi pointed out during the depression, "Industrial civilization in the United States seems to be constantly increasing the number condemned to dependency or parasitism."[8] Corporate industrial civilization produces confusion in people as to the meaning and importance of work. Workers band together in unions to protect their sense of purpose and dignity, yet their skills and sense of what should be produced are defined in terms of market valuations. In addition, it should be noted that it takes fewer people than ever before to produce more in American life, although bureaucracy has greatly increased. Whereas in the 1930s Borsodi judged some 40 percent of the population to being involved in some aspect of productive work, if we were to use the same criteria today, the number has dropped to less than one-third of the total population.

Part of the myth of the middle class during the period of the cold war was the belief that Americans were no longer primarily manual workers. It was comforting to believe that the majority of workers had become white collar workers and that Americans worked with their brains or were salesmen whose missionary task was to sell a better life through consumer goods. The reason that people embraced this view is obvious. It is hard to admit that a majority of the work population spend their lives in brutal places like factories. It was more comfortable to believe that factory work was being automated out with the conclusion that workers were getting better jobs than those they held in factories.[9]

Burdened with so many myths, the working class has found itself unable to form its own ideology or in Marxist terms, its own class consciousness. The onslaught from the great corporations, the packaging of achievement dreams through films, schools, and churches, and the pattern of state socialist brutality stopped any such consciousness from forming. Of course, class consciousness is of a different character in the United States than in Europe.

During the late nineteenth century, the labor movement in the United States (the Knights of Labor, for example) reflected much more of a petty bourgeois anarchist form. Workers built their strength from small producer cooperatives and producer workshops. This meant that families owning farms, small shopkeepers, or independent craftsmen worked day and night in order to keep out of the mass labor force and factories as dependent employees. Such consciousness became materially irrelevant as the great corporations captured more and more of the industrial and distribution process. In addition, consciousness took the form of the radical protection of individual actions. The Socialist Party and the Communist Party in the United States both failed to understand the mentality of Americans who saw themselves as hyperindividualistic and hypervoluntaristic. The corporate collectivist covered his demands for productive and profit efficiency through division of labor with obeisance to the myth of individualism and making it.

National unions were ineffective in the face of the collectivization of the work process by corporations until union organizing was given official blessings in Section 7a of the National Recovery Act. Leftist organizers tied their stars to John L. Lewis, but by 1940 his own role in the CIO was contained by the steelworkers. In 1949-50 unions dominated by the Left were expelled from the CIO as more conservative leadership emerged. The argument used against the Left and the so-called communist-dominated unions was that they sought to promote the interests of the Soviet Union and of communism and they could not be trusted with national security plans for war materials and defense contracts. The leaders of the nine unions branded communist-dominated were doomed once they supported Henry Wallace and the Progressive Party in the presidential election in 1948. When Wallace did badly at the polls, it was easy to arrange expulsion of the leftist unions from the CIO.[10] The social democratic labor leaders who replaced the

pro-Wallace labor leaders were coopted into the national security system and used by the government
for special purposes. For example, the Reuthers were
active with the CIA in Europe during the days of the
Marshall Plan, and Arnold Zander, the president of
the Municipal Employees Union, spread funds to
other unions for CIA projects during his tenure;
Joseph Beirne of the Communications Workers
Union did the same. And former Communist Party
leaders like Jay Lovestone thrived in the bureaucracy of the AFL-CIO hierarchy. They continued to
settle their old scores of a generation. But now it was
done with official sanction and encouragement of the
CIA, AID, and the National Security Council.
Domestically, the unions retained privileged status
over the unorganized. But even with such privileges,
most families were only one paycheck away from
disaster.

Franz Oppenheimer, the political scientist, points
out that in any modern constitutional state, each
class attempts to obtain as much of the share of production as possible.[11] Obviously, this results in class
conflict unless the economic pie can grow. Thus, armaments buildups play an important role because
they create internal production for imperial and undefined purposes. Workers bought into the national
security state system as did bureaucrats because they
saw the possibility of a better and more exciting personal life through official actions, and, thus, their
economic livelihood was assured. In a general sense,
economists were able to say growth increased even
though the types of growth in any strict analysis of
social cost accounting were wasteful and rather sad.
Labor and production were being put to antihumane
purposes. It is impossible to say that missiles and

nuclear weapons had redeeming social value like the great cathedrals of the Middle Ages. Indeed, they serve quite another master. Nevertheless, jobs were created which touched people's need for work, their patriotism, and the playful, extraordinary minds of scientists and engineers. The national security state sought to mask class conflict (who got what out of national production). That this intention was hidden behind the flag of patriotism or the lab coats of scientists did not change the fact that great resources were being expended for the interests of the business and military elite with the support of the scientists.

In business terms, the national security state apparatus has done little to encourage small business. As the staff economist of the Joint Economic Committees has pointed out: "In 1976, the 100 largest defense contractors received 28.9 billion dollars in contract awards, amounting to 69.0 percent of the total awarded. The top ten contractors received nearly half of the value awarded to the top 100 and approximately 31 percent of all awards." [12] From time to time, new groups of businessmen are thrust forward through accidents of capital accumulation as in farming, for example. Most local businessmen, however, understand that the state's regulatory intervention is used as a mechanism to protect the large corporations against the small ones and that the regulations required are negotiated between the largest businesses and the government to the disadvantage of smaller firms.

There were recessions in 1949, 1958-60, and 1973-75, but the postwar period was one which Americans saw as a time of prosperity. Nevertheless, the question of who benefited from the national security state should be carefully analyzed. The South and Southwest gained enormously from the arms race and various wars and interventions. New Deal programs had not developed these regions because large infusions of capital were not forthcoming from either the public or private sector. Following World War II, there was no impetus in Congress or the bureaucracy to implement the 1938 New Deal regional development plan for the South because it would have required direct federal interference in local class structures, threatening the power of the plantation elites, and breaking the wretched local laws and customs against blacks. Instead, this region developed itself through the emergence of defense and high technology industries subsidized by the federal government. The use and expansion of military bases in the South also brought economic growth to small businesses which depended on such bases.

The salutatory economic changes which occurred in the South and Southwest related to the increased value of natural gas and oil, the military tradition which encouraged national enterprises that were of a military nature, black migration to northern cities, and the willingness of blacks to force the desegregation issue without making basic demands on the economic system itself. Of course, workers have found themselves tied to the national security state even though cities suffered and few gains were made in the area of social services. Because of the nature of the public reality and the fact that the public spaces were dominated by the ideologies of those at the top of the pyramidal society, the subjective sensibilities, private problems, and personal needs of most people could hardly be heard or attended. Thirty years after its formation, we find the national security state exacerbates the economic crises. Those at the top of the corporations are ambiguous about their purposes and class interests. They are often specialists who understand things in compartmentalized ways as compared to the older ruling elites of thirty years ago who had a clearer consciousness of what was needed and what was intended. The older elites knew that the state was necessary for their survival against the poor and against each other. Corporate managers do not have a clear consciousness of how to rule in a way which will convince their children and wives who are exposed to other ideas. To make matters more unsettling, the children of the ruling elite are not solidly part of their parents' value structure. These young people do not have the same ethics that their parents had thirty years ago. They are soft about being committed to achieving, getting ahead, dividing time into moments of preparation for other moments, or receiving cash in exchange for human time. They have become aware of the limited opportunities which a contracting internal economy affords them.

As in other nations, the middle class in the United States is composed of different layers. There are the lawyers and the doctors who often operate as individual entrepreneurs and the petty bourgeois or storekeepers who are small business operators. Unless they are financially clever, most of the income of those in the middle class is consumed in daily living. They buy services including education and health care which in other advanced capitalist states in Western Europe have long been seen as matters of the welfare state right. They are dependent on salary and expense accounts of corporations to whom they are indentured. Doctors and lawyers have been the most successful in sustaining themselves. Many of them syndicate or incorporate to buy property and hope for propertied status which is not dependent on their daily work. As the Marxists have said, there is a limit to what one is able to earn from the sweat of one's brow. There are few limits to income when it is from the sweat of others. However, most of the members of the middle class in the United States are little more than landless peasants with phenomenal indebtedness.

The state built a whole economy around armies and knowledge relating to armaments. Corporations developed an imperial style of services in which the poorer people service the richer people. The national pistol culture and the national extravagance system which the national security state encouraged directly contradicted the egalitarian side of citizenship and nationhood. Yeomanry and independence require a nonservice mentality; they require cooperative independence. The growth economy built around leisure, extravagance, and militarism hardly fits democratic practice. The attempt to make consumer goods the great leveler of taste and aspiration has failed. The maldistribution of wealth, income, and power cannot be hidden by overstocked stores with people trying to figure out how to be servants to others so they can survive. It has broken the working class in the United States and caused great malaise and boredom in the society and a pornographic interest in violence.

The value to the cities of the United States of empire has been very limited. There have been important decisions made by the armed forces which show how the population is experimented with and how it is held hostage. In the first case, there are examples of causing viruses and bacteria being tested on the population by the chemical corps of the U.S. Army and other Defense Department groups. The other case, more complicated but equally egregious, is the use of a countervalue and counter-force defense with nuclear weapons and missiles which, if used against the state's opponents, endangers the entire civilization of the United States.

The public life of the cities and their possibilities as organic liveable units are damaged by the imperial adventure. It required capital in the form of taxation, labor in the form of turning the attention of the middle class to abstract and glorious adventures in which they thought they were sharing, and an identification with imperial pursuits which could never match the dull work of making alleys a decent place for children to play or making buildings places in which people could live and work. The intellectual energy which existed went into the moon shots, the Indochina War, making nuclear weapons, paving highways to escape the cities, and constructing imperial structures like the Rayburn Office Building or the FBI Building.

It is well to look at some of the so-called national security successes in foreign policy with a critical eye. After all, these successes were supposedly meant to satisfy the old people in Dubuque and the Mississippi tenant farmers and fill them with pride and patriotic identification with the state and the exploits of its bureaucratic knights. Suppose you were a manufacturer in the Midwest, a man of affairs who even once held a position of trust in the government. What would you think of the last generation? What would your private thoughts be? During this period of time, China was lost and its leadership had to be recognized on its own terms by a man who rose to power by berating the U.S. loss in China. The Korean War was fought to a standstill even though the United States committed 475,000 troops at one time and 47,000 U.S. troops were killed there. To obtain the support of the United Nations General Assembly, Dean Acheson invented the Uniting for Peace Resolution which gave small nations power to act on matters which were originally reserved for the great states. Now this resolution is cited by Cuba and other nations in support of armed struggles in Africa. The Indochina War was lost with another 60,000 U.S. troops killed and 250,000 wounded. The anticommunists lost Portugal where the political struggle is a choice between socialism and communism. Americans were long proud of the 1962 Cuban Missile Crisis when the strategy of the Executive Committee of the National Security Council got the "other fellow" to blink (Rusk's phrase). But after blinking, what did the Soviets do? They began a large strategic military program to rival our own. Since such programs come to fruition between seven and fifteen years after they are initiated, the Soviets now appear to approach genocidal parity with the United States on the strategic level. The United States has little choice but to accept Castro's Cuba. The Cuban intervention in Angola had the support of the United Nations General Assembly, and the CIA was stopped by a handful of junior members of Congress.

The military aid given to various military leaders in Latin America which trained them in the ways of the U.S. military and suited them up with U.S. organizational structure and weaponry has resulted in anti-United States nationalism in Peru and shockingly even in Pinochet's Chile. In Italy the only way that the Christian Democratic Party and the capitalist class are able to function in the long run is by forming a coalition with the Communist Party.

The French government is also hostage to the Left. Once the Communist Party is included in the French Left, the Left coalition extends to over half of the electorate.

An imperialist would have to agree that the two trillion dollars spent on the military and military aid to keep U.S. imperial hegemony in its old form has been shaken. Even island nations like Trinidad baldly call for the independence of U.S. colony Puerto Rico without fear of reprisal. These questions are now asked privately in the high councils of government; they will soon be asked in the bars, church groups, and Rotary Clubs as well. Why are we spending all of this money? Why are we doing all of these things? These two questions now require the national security state to justify its existence in new ways. No doubt some presidential advisers will echo Graham Allison who would purge the entire permanent government. He called for a

> modern version of Thomas Jefferson's prescription of a little revolution every generation. This modern equivalent would call for a one-time revolution disestablishing the national security establishment: abolishing all departments, agencies, and coordinating mechanisms, and honorably discharging all members of the Permanent Government (who would be disqualified from serving in the next decade). Congress and the President would then proceed to fashion a new Executive branch, composed of new people aimed at current and future problems.[13]

But such ideas are technocratic fantasies. The state has to work at getting people to internalize the principle of imperialism and the view that any loss of empire is their personal loss. When government officials say that they want to restore a belief in the government's credibility, they usually mean that they want the individual citizen to share the government's consciousness and perception of reality. Political leaders are required to tell the people that a loss to Xerox or IBM or the failure of the CIA in its covert operations represents a loss of their freedom and unique existence. This is a critical task that a president is supposed to perform for a ruling elite. The reason that the Indochina War was so important was that for the first time since the Civil War, most people realized that the state's defeat might really be society's victory.

There is now a shattered consciousness which tends to show the average citizen that neither imperialism nor the national security state nor their leadership has been related to their everyday needs and aspirations. In 1975 the antiwar movement in the United States could have said that the society won when U.S. military troops withdrew from Vietnam. The movement should have taken partial credit for that victory. Having won, the question should have been asked, "Who were the opponents?" It is here that the differences would have become clear. The battle was between the assumptions and organization of the national security state and the people.

NOTES

1. John Morton Blum, ed., *The Price of Vision: The Diary of Henry A. Wallace, 1942-1946* (Boston: Houghton Mifflin Co., 1973), pp. 32 and 411; also see Barton J. Bernstein, ed., *Politics and Policies of the Truman Administration* (Chicago: Quadrangle Books, Inc., 1970).

2. Arthur J. Goldberg, *AFL-CIO: Labor United* (New York: McGraw-Hill, 1956), p. 183 and pp. 177-87.

3. James J. Matles and James Higgins, *Them and Us* (New York: Prentice-Hall, Inc., 1974).

4. Ibid., p. 138.

5. Ibid.

6. Lester C. Thurow, "Popular Mechanics: The Redistribution of Wealth," *Working Papers*, vol. 3, no. 4, 1976, pp. 23-27.

7. Francis Brown, "The Storm Center of the Banking Bills," in *The New Deal*, ed. Carl Degler (Chicago: Quadrangle Books, 1970), pp. 184-86. *Eccles'* quote in *The New York Times Magazine* 5 May 1935.

8. Ralph Borsodi, *Prosperity and Security* (New York: Harper Brothers, 1939), p. 129.

9. Andrew Levison, *The Working Class Majority* (New York: Coward, McCann and Geoghegan, 1974).

10. The unions expelled included the following: United Office and Professional Workers of America; Food, Tobacco, Agricultural and Allied Workers of America; National Union of Marine Cooks and Stewards; American Communications Association; International Fur and Leather Workers Union; International Longshoreman and Warehouseman's Union; International Union of Mine, Mill and Smelter Workers; United Public Workers of America; and International Fisherman and Allied Workers of America.

11. Franz Oppenheimer, *The State* (1914; reprint ed., New York: Free Life Editions, 1975), pp. 88-91.

12. Figures released by Department of Defense, OASD (Comptroller), Directorate for Information Operations and Control, 22 November 1976.

13. Graham T. Allison, "The Management of Defense and Arms Control Issues," in *Appendices: Commission on the Organization of Government*, vol. 4, p. 4.

4
The National Security State and the Rule of Law

The national security state has had a civilized gloss. Throughout this generation, it attempted to steer between fascism and socialism at home; it attempted to develop and establish a principle between extremes. To do so, it took over the assumptions of authoritarianism. We might say that the national security state was the compromise between Max Weber and Allen Dulles. It was a way of ordering things, men, and events into an understandable and predictable pattern. If there were dirty deals, only certain men did them or were in the chain. The deeds were closely held, as Kissinger would say, and kept under cover. Through the use of a system of masking or plausible denial, the state sought to preserve a form of legitimacy in the world even though the legitimacy itself was based on pomp, fraud, power, people's forgetfulness, and the narrow attention span of most of us. In its daily operations, the national security state sought a means of reproducing the same interests and world view, the same ideas in institutional and material form. Thus, the AEC produced bombs and the FBI produced undercover agents. Throughout the period of 1947-77, the national security state operated against the society's poorer classes whose demands invariably seem unruly and dangerous. This state also brought down power graspers who did not pay their just due to the bureaucratic apparatus and who attempted to change the accepted modes of giving and taking orders or destroy established sources of economic power. Nixon was seen, for example, as a putschist by such men of old wealth as Elliott Richardson. On the other hand, agency heads feared a presidential takeover of a bureaucracy which he believed was loyal to programs and not to his will. Nixon was a victim of a bureaucratic and baronial coup against his own attempt to purge the government during his second administration. Nixon found himself commanding a national security state which was unraveling because of the Indochina War. He found that it had not steered a centrist path between totalitarian ideologies. However, there was no way for this suspicious and insecure arriviste to lead the state and the baronial institutions back to the centrism of Eisenhower.

How are we to explain the state to the people? Norman Mailer's kaleidoscopic fantasy which brought the Mafia, the CIA, the media, the Kennedys, Nixon, and Marilyn Monroe together in some sort of horrible dance has turned out to be a more accurate picture of the way things operate than the models of the state learned in schools of public administration.

During the cold war period, the president and his immediate entourage became the brokers for the illegitimate power wielded by the CIA, the FBI, and the various gangs within them. They also sought to use these groups for their own purposes. The powerful seek maximum flexibility for their objectives. Ad hoc committees threaded the line between legitimacy, illegality, and crime.[1] Much of the time of the president and his advisors was spent curbing or ratifying the excesses of lower level bureaucrats emboldened by the imperial stance and the shroud of secrecy.[2] Thus, for example, after the CIA's failure at the Bay of Pigs, the president, the attorney general, and McGeorge Bundy undertook to control the national security bureaucracy through Maxwell Taylor and presidentially appointed committees. This so-called reform more deeply implicated the presidency in paramilitary and criminal affairs.

It should be noted that the entire framework of maximum flexibility for leaders and the national security bureaucracy is meant to encompass both domestic and foreign activity. The control techniques which presidents used during war and cold war against the poor and the subversives at home and which had been transported abroad during the cold war were also used against the middle classes, the bureaucracies, and the leaders of the major political parties.

The FBI and other police agencies of the federal government proceeded to enforce the Procrustean bed of antileftist conformist ideology both inside and outside the government. President Truman's Executive Order 9835 issued in March 1947 required loyalty oaths of government officials.[3] Many who held positions in institutions such as labor unions, universities, and the media were purged. By 1949 they found themselves eliminated from policy debates on the character of American society or treated as objects of contempt or of benign tolerance. (As we shall see, the nature of the debate which came to take on

new and surprising forms in the 1960s was not contemplated by the national security state and its apparatus.) The effects of the Truman loyalty probes
and those later undertaken by Senator Joseph
McCarthy and J. Edgar Hoover were to enforce a view
of the world based on hatred of communism and to
prepare an automatic defense of corporate capitalism
as the reason for U.S. prosperity and the justification
for U.S. military adventures and alliances, both
covert and overt. To this end, the national security
state was dedicated.

In *Powers of Government*, Bernard Schwartz outlines three fundamental elements of the rule of law:
"1) the absence of arbitrary power; 2) The subjugation
of the State and its officers to the ordinary law; and 3)
The recognition of basic principles superior to the
State itself." [4] The assumption of Schwartz and others
is that the rule of law is crucial to the existence of
representative democracy. Even for the radical revolutionary Thomas Paine, the law was king. As he
said, "Let a crown be placed thereon, by which the
world may know that, so far as we approve of monar-
chy, that in America *the law is king*." [5]

The national security state and the rule of law are
mortal enemies. In the first place, by its nature and
its mission, the national security state apparatus
needs arbitrary power. Such power has its own code
which is meant to govern or justify the behavior of the
initiated after the fact. It operates to protect the state
apparatus from the citizenry. In its defensive form, it
is hidden under instant and specious doctrines such
as executive privilege. [6] This apparatus seeks to cede
to the discretion of officials the power of the citizens to
manage their future or participate with others in that
management. Government officials attempt to con-

trol the kinds of politics and citizen activities which they do not favor. They see no distinctions among geographic boundaries and are apt to operate in essentially the same way against both Americans and non-Americans. Thus, the attempt of the CIA to assassinate Patrice Lumumba in the Congo is directly analogous to the FBI's attempt to politically destroy Martin Luther King, Jr., in the United States. President Nixon's sanction of the decisions of the forty Committee to intervene and attempt to prevent the election of Allende through bribe offers and other means is strikingly similar to the methods CREEP used in Nixon's reelection campaign or to methods used against the United States Socialist Workers Party.[7]

The police agencies have attempted to serve as a brake on the political process. The COINTELPRO programs of the FBI have employed an astonishing variety of means to disrupt the activities of groups which sought to exercise their participatory rights. Programs like Operation Hoodwink were meant, for example, to incite organized crimes against the Communist Party, to entrap war objectors into undertaking bombings as in the case of the Camden, New Jersey draft board affair, and to break up human and social relations by sending forged documents and threatening letters to victims of federal and local police enterprises.[8]

Break-ins, burglaries, wiretaps, and buggings on the citizenry have been a central aspect of the work of the FBI as they have undertaken to humiliate, ridicule, and harass civil rights workers, antiwar groups, radicals, conservatives, and any group which did not share the assumptions or the influence of those in charge.[9] In addition, the CIA has taken pride in training local police in bugging, photo surveillance, and surreptitious entry.[10] These incidents are reminiscent of the struggles in Italy under Mussolini in the 1920s. Indeed, it may be said that the virus of totalitarianism has spread from one nation to another in the twentieth century with no exception granted to the United States.

> An important fact [in the case of Mussolini's Italy] is that the fascist squadrons had at their disposal ... not only the subsidies of their financial backers but the material and moral support of the repressive forces of the state: police, carabinieri, and army. The police recruited for the squadrons. urging outlaws to enroll in them and promising them all sorts of benefits and immunity. The police loaned their cars to squadron members, and rejected applications for arms permits by workers and peasants while extending the permits granted to fascists. The guardians of "law and order" had their orders to remain idle when the fascists attacked the "reds" and to intervene only if the latter resisted. Often the police collaborated with the fascists in preparing attacks on labor organizations.[11]

This description of fascist strategy in Italy in 1921 is striking in its resemblance to the approach used by the CIA, Kissinger, Nixon, and McCone in their successful attempt at bringing down the Marxist government of Allende in Chile:

> a) Collect intelligence on coup-minded officers; b) Create a coup climate by propaganda, disinformation, and terrorist activities intended to provoke the left to give a pretext for a coup: (Cable 611, Hq. to Sta. 10/7/70); c) Inform those coup-minded officers that the U.S. government would give them full support in a coup short of direct U.S. military intervention.[12]

The line between criminal gangs and the police is often crossed in the national security state. The purposes may appear obscure to the average law-abiding citizen, but the process of tyranny can be felt by the body politic which finds reason and justice suspended for power and domination.[13]

> One FBI provocateur resigned when he was asked to arrange the bombing of a bridge in such a way that the person who placed the booby-trapped bomb would be killed. This was in Seattle where it was revealed that FBI infiltrators had been engaged in a campaign of arson, terrorism, and bombing of university and civil buildings, and where the FBI arranged a robbery, entrapping a young black man who was paid $75 for the job and killed in a police ambush.

The *San Diego Union*, on 10 January 1976, reported that the secret army organization which fire-bombed cars, burglarized the homes of antiwar protestors, and ransacked offices was "a centrally designed and externally financed infrastructure designed for terror and sabotage." According to the *San Diego Union*, the acts took place during 1971-72 and were "sanctioned by the nation's most powerful and highly respected law enforcement agency, the Federal Bureau of Investigation."[14] This allegation, however, has been denied by the FBI.[15]

The attempt by holders of arbitrary power to prevent people from exercising their participatory rights is invariably accompanied by forms of personal harrassment against people who have no interest in the exercise of their rights. Their interest is limited to carrying on the ordinary functions of life. Here the arbitrary power of the national security apparatus operates in a less obvious, more automatic, and less obtrusive way. We see the building of files on a person which are used to engage in blackmail or to control possibilities of future employment for the object-victim. This course of bureaucratic behavior is especially popular in a period when bureaucracies grow larger, computers more sophisticated, and leaderships more insecure. It is punctuated with predictable danger in that vying leadership elites use police and other records as weapons to destroy their opponents or settle old scores. Such activities are common practice in the bureaucracy of the national and internal security apparatus.[16] There is nothing in public law which sets limits for the FBI or which suggests that authority exists for carrying on its comprehensive surveillance activities in the area of so-called subversive activities.[17]

In the dual state, specifically rejected by U.S. law, "legal concepts are not applicable to the political sphere, which is regulated by arbitrary measures, in which the dominant officials exercise unfettered discretionary perogatives."[18] The national security state is the U.S. version of the dual state. Within the national security agencies, we can discern several levels of paralegal and illegal activities.

At one level, the national security apparatus operates according to a paralegal structure which has its own administrative and self-justifying system. It is private, in the sense that it has its own standards. Thus, the now famous Forty Committee is an example of an attempt to draw the various police, military, and criminal forces at the command of the leadership into a private and self-justifying administrative system. "Beginning in 1955, the responsibility for authorizing CIA covert action operations lay with the Special Group, a sub-committee of the National Security Council (NSC) composed of the President's Assistant for National Security Affairs, the Director of Central Intelligence, the Deputy Secretary of Defense and the Undersecretary of State for Political Affairs."[19] Today this group, known as the Forty Committee, once was expanded to include the Chairman of the Joint Chiefs of Staff. This part of the national security apparatus operates according to its own rules and regulations and takes little or no account of public law and asserts its own definition of national security and national interest (a definition which is invariably oriented toward the ruling class). We may refer to it as "lightly covered" because it may or may not surface from time to time, as in the case of the Forty Committee. When it does surface, it seeks to justify its actions by embracing principles of positive law and of the dual state.

On another level, the national security state carries on activities which are flatly illegal. At this level criminal behavior becomes an important operational instrument. National Security Defense Memorandum 40 issued in 1970 points out that the intelligence apparatus must be ready for all contingencies and have responses basically researched and in existence.[20] In other words, preparing for criminality and involving or nurturing criminal behavior must be part of the costs of the national security state since it is never clear when criminality will prove useful. This includes forgery and counterfeiting, assassination, and the employment of known criminals.

> CIA must necessarily be responsible for planning. Occasionally suggestions for action will come from outside sources but, to depend entirely on such requirements would be an evasion of the Agency's responsibilities.

Also, the average person, both in government and out-side, is *thinking along normal lines* and to develop clan-destine cold war activities properly, persons knowing both the capabilities and limitations of clandestine ac-tion must be studying and devising how such actions can be undertaken effectively.[21]

This kind of thinking goes beyond the paralegal procedure. It gives rise to plans and actions of a frightful nature. An unlimited choice of means has been extended to agents or hired contract officers. Thus, the sober William Colby planned and carried out the Phoenix Program which resulted in the kil-ling of some 20,000 Vietnamese. They were killed because they were ostensibly part of the "Viet Cong's infrastructure."[22]

Another criminally-oriented policy maker was the imaginative General Lansdale. He was put in charge of the MONGOOSE program to overthrow Castro through covert means. He recommended exploiting the potential of the underworld in Cuban cities to harass and bleed the community control apparatus. Added to this plan was another suggestion (among thirty-one other planning tasks) to utilize biological and chemical warfare against the Cuban sugar crop workers.[23] (It should be noted that such activities are proscribed by international law and would be so treated under the Personal Accountability Bill intro-duced by thirty-eight members of the Ninety-fourth Congress.)[24]

The minutes of the Special Group on 19 June 1963 suggest the manner in which the executive under-took war and warlike activities and pulled itself and the government in unaccountable policy crimes. At a meeting in which McNamara, General Hee, Harri-man, McCone, Desmond Fitzgerald of the CIA, and

McGeorge Bundy were present, a sabotage program was presented by the CIA to the members of the special group. It was to be directed at "four major segments of the Cuban economy" including electric power, petroleum refineries and storage facilities, railroad and highway transportation, and production and manufacturing. Raids were to be conducted from outside Cuba using Cuban agents under CIA control. Missions would be staged from a United States key.[25]

Here we have officers of the government who have statutorily defined responsibilities in the constitutional order acting in their hidden role as officers of the dual state. They cannot be reached or controlled through constitutional or legal means. At the first meeting of the National Security Council in December 1947, covert operations were authorized thus giving the go ahead to criminal action.[26] It would take us too far afield to analyze the social class bias of the views held by this and other executive committees which assume a consensus by the members of the government for carrying out of actions against underprivileged and powerless people. What are we to make of Ambassador Korry who said that once Allende the Marxist was elected president, the United States would "do all within our power to condemn Chile and the Chileans to utmost deprivation and poverty . . ."?[27] What are we to make of President Nixon and Secretary of State Kissinger who, having been emboldened by various multinational corporations including IT&T and PEPSICO, pursued another attempt to bring down Allende (an attempt which was operated through the White House and even kept secret from the Forty Committee)?[28] According to Kissinger, this plan involved a group that was unknown to others for reasons of security and charged with the responsibility of working with the Chilean military in bringing about a coup against Allende.[29] They succeeded, of course. Suffice it to say that the consensus which existed fifteen years ago among elites no longer exists. And more to the point, this consensus is no longer shared by the American people.

The cultural hegemony in which all classes internalized the world view of the ruling elite has been broken as it had to be in a democracy. It is no wonder that this hegemony has been broken for the rule of law is challenged directly by the operators of the state. Thus, for example, former Vice-President Nelson Rockefeller paid an average of 10 percent tax on his total income, an amount approximately equal to the amount paid by the average worker who earns $8,000 a year.[30] Simultaneously, as chairman of the commission to investigate the CIA, Rockefeller attempted to legitimize the paralegal activity of the national security apparatus by turning crime into law. In his guise as statesman, Rockefeller was representative of those oligarchs who believe in weak legislatures and favor government by authorities who are responsible to no elected officials or legislatures but to the most powerful economic and military elements in the society.[31]

According to Justice Brandeis, "at the foundation of our civil liberties lies the principle which denies to government officials an exceptional position before the law and which accepts the same rules of conduct that are commands to the citizen."[32] Accordingly, everyone is subject to the ordinary law and amenable to the rules of the courts. Ostensibly, this would be the one means of guarding against the dual state. The role of the courts, however, is exceedingly limited with regard to the national security apparatus thus permitting the expansion of its paralegal and illegal activities. When examining the decisions of the courts, we know that the judiciary has handled few cases involving the CIA or the National Security Agency (NSA). The courts are frightened of the dual state and hope that the problem will go away if it is disregarded. Furthermore, when such cases have been presented to the courts, judges have been reluctant or unable for institutional reasons to rule against the secret agencies or inquire about their activities.[33]

Why does the doctrine of *Marbury* v. *Madison* stop at the gates of Langley, Virginia? One reason is that secret agencies specialize in lying. Indeed, they are so structured by mission and organization as to give credence to the view that in as much as they are the children of Allen Dulles and J. Edgar Hoover, they are also the descendants of Epimenides. A stock in trade of the CIA has been plausible denial. This doctrine is meant to protect operatives "from the consequences of disclosures" and "to mask decisions of the President and his senior staff members."[34] The masking process is "designed to allow the President and other senior officials to deny knowledge of an operation should it be disclosed."[35] In other words, plausible denial is a doctrine which encouraged the invention of false information or lies which will be acceptable to other government agencies, the courts, the public, and competing or uninformed groups within the secret agencies themselves. Related to the doctrine of plausible denial is the need to know principle. The operational effect of this principle is, as Richard Barnet has said, the need not to know.[36] In other words, the FBI and the CIA operate on the basis that various groups within their own agencies including higher officials have little idea of what others in the same chain of command are doing.

However, democracy and its operative principle, the rule of law, require a ground on which to stand. That ground, as former President Ford said when he was sworn in as president, is truth.[37] In this regard, the government has a higher duty to tell the truth than the citizen because it is the government which embodies the tradition and values of the body politic. When the government lies or is so structured as to permit only lies and self-deception, it is clear that the governing process and the organization of power has become some form other than that generally understood by the citizenry as the original constitutional form. The doctrines of plausible denial and the need to know present problems of particular significance for the judiciary as enforcer of the rule of law. With the development of the national security state, the duty of telling the truth has been substantially waived. Indeed, it is taken for granted that lies and masks are the official's tools for group and self-protection.

One example of the kind of falsification that is routine within the national security apparatus is the GATTO incident. Against orders, the U.S.S. GATTO drifted within one mile of the Soviet coast. A Soviet sub rammed the GATTO somewhere between the Straits and the White Sea. The GATTO was ready to fire a nuclear missile at the Russian sub, but the GATTO escaped without needing to do so. The officers of the ship were requested to file two sets of reports. One set was to consist of six copies of descriptions of the incident as it actually occurred; the other set was to be twenty-five copies falsifying the incident. The Pentagon admitted filing the falsified reports, but said that it filed the true report with the Forty Committee. However, when interviewed, officials could not locate or remember any reports about the GATTO.[38] There have been at least four midocean collisions between United States Navy and Soviet nuclear-powered submarines carrying nuclear weapons since the mid-1960s. These were ostensibly intelligence operations which could have easily resulted in nuclear disaster.[39]

Since unacceptable acts (that is, actions that are constitutionally, legally, or morally questionable) are denied by the agencies as a matter of course, there has been no way for the courts to test the veracity of statements made by the secret agencies. For example, how are we to know when the FBI engaged in a particular course of the conduct such as wiretapping, burglary, or entrapment? We now learn that the FBI kept at least two separate sets of books. One set which is available to the courts reflects the FBI's so-called acceptable or legitimate purposes. The other set is unknown except to the initiated.[40] To the extent that the second set is recorded, it apparently shows the actual operations of the FBI and special groups and their special missions and special purposes undertaken for themselves and for special friends. This, however, is not the record which the courts receive. *Marbury* is defeated by national security practice.

According to Schwartz, the third element of the rule of law is recognition that there are principles which are superior to the state itself. This is an important safeguard against legislatures that pass laws which may be criminal. It is also a justification for the citizenry to act in a civilly disobedient manner against laws or governmental acts which shock the conscience of the society. The history of the twentieth century is replete with paralegal orders for bombings, concentration camps, assassinations, and break-ins.[41] A citizen does not affirm or assent to every proclamation, law, or secret rule of a secret police agency whether it operates within the United States or abroad; a citizen does not affirm every executive order which appears to operate under the color of the law. Instead, we may discern limited assent which must be continuously won from the citizenry by the government. The government accomplishes this by doing justice and by recognizing human and natural rights.

These generally shared notions of human rights seem to be in a race against the inclinations of the national security state swollen with nuclear weapons. There exists a seeming willingness on the part of the bureaucracy, the military, and science to build and use weapons of mass destruction on hundreds of millions of people because they do not see the world in the same ways as does a rival set of leaders. This situation poses a question which cannot be dodged: what right does a state have to commit suicide for the people?[42] This issue has yet to be considered by the people, the Congress, or the courts.

One may ask whether the rule of law can begin to deal with any of these issues. What help can citizens expect to have if they raise the question of whether the state can commit suicide for the body politic through its policy of mindless armament or its use of nuclear weapons to destroy whole classes of people?

The courts have attempted to recognize the constitutional rights of the citizenry as they relate to equality of opportunity. They have also attempted to give proper credence to the civil rights of people. This objective, however, has not been shared by the police apparatus. Thus, throughout the period of the civil rights struggles of the 1960s, the FBI had the unfortunate habit of allowing the local police to beat and jail civil rights demonstrators. In addition, the FBI as well as the CIA infiltrated black nationalist groups in the ghetto for the specific purpose of ridiculing and discrediting their attempts to organize.[43] There was no recognition by the police agencies that the struggles of the civil rights movement were for natural and human rights. This is not surprising because to guarantee such rights would mean that their own activities would have to come under strict scrutiny and finally be dismantled in favor of local neighborhood and community police. It should be noted that, based on a study of the Media Papers, stolen from the files of the FBI in Media, Pennsylvania, 40 percent of the FBI's time is spent in harassing and keeping tabs on political groups which sought some measure of recognition of their rights.[44] It is hardly surprising that the national security apparatus, built as it is upon principles of unaccountability, secrecy, ultraallegiance to the state, and willingness to lie to the courts and legislatures, is unconcerned with human or natural rights.[45] (One may recall Ambassador Popper's attempt to criticize the Chilean Junta for disregarding human rights and torturing prisoners. Kissinger instructed Popper to stop giving the junta political science lessons.)[46]

Within the U.S. Constitution, however, there is the seed of a radical understanding of the rights of the people. Under the Ninth Amendment, the rights of the people cannot be disparaged (i.e., they cannot be disparaged by the government, the secret apparatus of the government, the gangs which operate within the secret apparatus, or the president in an effort to commit mass suicide). How is this process to be interrupted? It is only in a continuous dialogue from the grass roots that imperialism can be interrupted. Less than forty years ago, the antiimperialist Ludlow Resolution which almost became federal law stated that wars could not be declared without a referendum of the people.[47]

NOTES

1. R. Stavins, R. Barnet, and Marcus Raskin, *Washington Plans an Aggressive War*, pp. 194-252; *Covert Actions*, vol. 7 of *Hearings on Senate Resolution 21 Before the Senate Select Committee to Study Governmental Operations with Respect to Intelligence Activities*, 94th Cong., 1st sess., 1975, 1-136, 148-210.

2. Ibid.

3. U.S., Exec. Order No. 9835, 3 C.F.R. 627, 1943-48 Compilation.

4. Bernard Schwartz, *The Powers of Government* 26 (1963).

5. Thomas Paine, *Common Sense: Addressed to the Inhabitants of America (A New Edition 1776)*; in *Common Sense and Other Political Writings* 332, N. Atkins, 1953. *Common Sense* lays out the theory of natural rights, law, and independence which the new nation applauded. See generally C. Beard and M. Beard, *The Rise of American Civilization* 237, 2d ed. rev., 1947.

6. Alas, Chief Justice Burger in his opinion, *United States v. Nixon*, 418 U.S. 683 (1974), does nothing to limit either executive privilege or confidentiality. See generally, Cotter, "Legislative Oversight," in *Congress the First Branch* pp. 25, 55 ed. A. de Grazia, abr. ed. 1967.

7. Chomsky, "Introduction," in *COINTELPRO: The FBI's Secret War on Political Freedom* ed. C. Perkus, 1975, pp. 3-26; *Senate Select Committee to Study Governmental Operations with Respect to Intelligence Activities, Alleged Assassination Plots Involving Foreign Leaders S. 465*, 94th Cong., 1st Sess. 1975, pp. 19-67.

8. *COINTELPRO*, pp. 119-71, vol. 6 of *Federal Bureau of Investigation Hearings on Senate Resolution 21*, appendix 4, p. 1151.

9. *Hearings on FBI Counterintelligence Programs before the Civil Rights and Constitutional Rights Subcommittee of the House Committee on the Judiciary*, 93rd Cong., 2nd sess. 1974, pp. 10-47.

10. Ross, "Surreptitious Entry," in *The CIA File*, ed. Robert Borosage and John Marks (1976).

11. D. Guerin, *Fascism and Big Business* p. 98 (1939).

12. *Alleged Assassination Plots Involving Foreign Leaders*, p. 234.

13. Chomsky, p. 15.

14. *San Diego Union*, 10 January 1976; quoted in "Newspaper Says FBI Funded Terror Unit," *Washington Post*, 11 January 1976, p. A2.

15. "FBI Funded Terror Unit," *Washington Post*.

16. *Inquiry into the Destruction of former FBI Director J. Edgar Hoover's Files & FBI Recordkeeping, Hearing before a Subcommittee of the House Committee on Government Operations*, 94th Cong., 1st sess., 1975, 59, hereafter cited as *Hoover Files Hearings*.

17. *Mr. Nittle. Counsel of the House Committee on Internal Security*. Mr. Maroney, I see literally nothing specific in the directives of Presidents Roosevelt and Truman which informs us or the FBI as to the precise mission to be fulfilled by the Federal Government in undertaking investigations of subversive activities. Has this been spelled out in any other published or unpublished memoranda or directives?

Mr. Maroney. Deputy Assistant Attorney General. I think we are back to what we were talking about earlier as to particular directives to the Attorneys General from time to time.

Mr. Nittle. I see nothing in title 28, FCFR which informs us of the precise mission to be fulfilled. Wouldn't that help to inform the FBI of the scope and nature of the investigations to be undertaken?

Mr. Maroney. The FBI has its own manual. I am trying to tell you the Attorney General has from time to time provided them with instructions as to what to investigate and what to furnish the Department in this area, but it is not wrapped up in a nice little package.

Hearings on Domestic Intelligence Operations for Internal Security Purposes Before the House Committee on Internal Security, 93rd Cong., 2nd sess., 1974, pt 1, at 3446-48.

18. Schwartz.

19. *Alleged Assassination Plots Involving Foreign Leaders*, p. 10; see also *United States v. United States District Court*, 407 U.S. 297, 324 (1972).

20. Irving Howe and Lewis Coser, *The American Communist Party*, 2nd ed. (1962) p. 426.

21. Directive of the National Security Council, NSC 5412/2 in *Alleged Assassination Plots Involving Foreign Leaders*, p. 9, n. 4.

22. *The CIA File*, p. 190.

23. *Alleged Assassination Plots Involving Foreign Leaders*, pp. 139-69.

24. U.S., Congress, House, *H.R. 8388*, 94th Cong., 1st sess., 1975; a memorandum in explication of the bill containing a detailed analysis of its contents appears at 121 *Congressional Record* H6396, 8 July 1975.

25. Ibid., p. 173.

26. See NSC 5412/2.

27. *Alleged Assassination Plots Involving Foreign Leaders*, p. 231, n.2.

28. Ibid., p. 250.

29. Ibid., pp. 246-55.

30. Conflict of Interest Group, Institute for Policy Studies, "The Disability of Wealth, An Inquiry into the Nomination of Nelson Rockefeller as Vice-President" (an unpublished report available at the Institute for Policy Studies, 1909 Que St., N.W., Washington, D.C., 1974).

31. Ibid.

32. Quoted in Schwartz, *Alleged Assassination Plots Involving Foreign Leaders*, p. 9.

33. *Alfred A. Knopf, Inc. v. Colby*, 509 F.2d 1362 (4th Circuit Court 1975) cert. denied, 421 U.S. 922 (1974); Developments in the Law—The National Security Interest and Civil Liberties, 85 *Harvard Law Review*, pp. 1130, 1134 (1972).

34. *Alleged Assassination Plots Involving Foreign Leaders*, p. 11.

35. Ibid., pp. 11-12.

36. R. Stavins, R. Barnet and M. Raskin, *Washington Plans an Aggressive War*, p. 246.

37. Remarks of President Gerald R. Ford following his swearing in as twenty-eighth president of the United States, 10 Weekly Comp. of Pres. Doc. 1023, 1024, 9 August 1974.

38. Command Study Group, R. Staviñs, Chairman, Study on U.S.S. GATTO, Problems of Nuclear Accidents Four (February 1974) (unpublished report available at the Institute for Policy Studies, 1909 Que St., Washington, D.C., 1974).

39. Ibid., pp. 1-7.

40. *Hoover Files Hearings*, pp. 36-48.

41. F. Neumann, *Behemoth* (1942) pp. 452-58; T. Becker, *American Government, Past, Present, Future* p. 319 (1976); R. Stavins, R. Barnet and M. Raskin, *Washington Plans an Aggressive War* pp. 284-85 (explaining the use of paralaw).

42. Marcus Raskin, *Being and Doing*, pp. 47-76.

43. *COINTELPRO: The FBI's Secret War on Political Freedom*, pp. 9-17, 110-18.

44. Ibid.

45. Ibid.

46. *New York Times*, 28 September 1974, p. 9.

47. Marcus Raskin, *Notes on the Old System* (1974).

5
The National Security State and the Question of War

Before the Second World War, Roosevelt and his cabinet had already identified Indochina as a U.S. interest. This became one of the immediate causes of the Second World War when the Japanese decided to move into Indochina against the Vichy French. The Japanese occupied established military bases there on 25 July 1941, and in retaliation, the United States froze all Japanese assets in the United States the following day. This freeze ended all trade with the Japanese. The United States further served notice that the Japanese were to give up their plans for a new order in Asia and return the Indochinese area to the French. This prewar demand dictated the outlines of U.S. policy at the end of the Second World War.

The United States acquiesced in de Gaulle's decision to take back Indochina as part of the French empire. This was an expensive decision for both France and the United States. The U.S. aid program to France after the war was less than the cost of the French colonial war in Indochina. According to Secretary of State Acheson, the war against the Viet

103

Minh cost the French between one-third and one-half of their national budget. After 1950 the United States continued to subsidize the French attempt to restore its hegemony over Indochina but explicitly as a U.S. deputy and as part of its global strategy to contain communism. U.S. leaders including Dulles and Bedell Smith supported the French and Vietnamese colonial forces, fearing that the independence movement of Ho Chi Minh would feed the emergence of liberation forces throughout the world, forces which the bureaucrats, military officers, and corporate leaders could not understand, and thus feared.

In 1954 the United States acquiesced in Mendes-France's peace settlement with Ho although the United States would not sign the agreement. The United States did acknowledge the French settlement, and in exchange, the French Assembly was persuaded to support Dulles' position of bringing Germany into the European Defense Community. After 1954 the French were out of the picture as the deputy of the United States, a position they held for four bitter years, 1950-54. By 1961 a military reason for direct U.S. involvement was invented in the national security planning bureaucracy. The U.S. military wanted to test its weapons and brush fire war concepts. Indochina was chosen as a proving ground in the same way that the Spanish Civil War played that role between the Axis and the Soviet Union. Policy planners like Eugene Staley authored the Staley-Taylor Plan to test the "strategic hamlet" theory of moving the South Vietnamese peasant population into 17,000 compounds. When the intervention was defended by its bureaucratic proponents to a reluctant Congress, it was rationalized as a global strategy which would uphold the free world.

The State Department said that the U.S. involvement was no different from the actions that were taken in Greece, Turkey, Korea, and Guatemala (supposedly more popular with Congress).

While the military was caught in sublimited war plans, U.S. leaders were caught in mindless expansion and delusional concern with the prestige of the United States. President Johnson often told the people that the United States sought no territory nor had selfish interests. It wanted to intervene in Vietnam because it was the right thing to do. U.S. policy fell quickly into the classic definition of imperialism as described by Schumpeter, "the objectless disposition on the part of the State to unlimited forcible expansion." Once having expanded, a state will fight to maintain its irrational expansion. When opponents of the war complained about it, the response of the U.S. policy maker was invariably grounded in the language of the so-called "defense of civilization" or the "free world." Lower level bureaucrats were expected to withhold their critical faculties and embrace the U.S. military enterprise. The more callous, such as William Sullivan, rose quickly in the bureaucracy as difficult and dirty jobs needed doing.

Ostensibly, a fundamental purpose of a bureaucratic apparatus in national security and foreign affairs is to weed out wild schemes in favor of ordinary and somewhat humdrum processes and policies. This objective can only work when there are etched legal boundaries which the state will not cross and when agencies of the state will not compete with other agencies for entrance. This objective cannot be achieved if the leadership constantly seeks new frontiers, or bureaucratic agencies seek modes of expansion in order to justify their existence. Once leadership seeks new frontiers and bureaucracies seek expansion, it is not possible to limit imperial appetite. Each new weapon, every technological breakthrough, military tactic, or popular cultural phase become grist for the perpetuation of expansion. In Indochina U.S. presidents made commitments which other presidents thought they were required to uphold, and national security agencies such as the Defense Department, AID, and the CIA nurtured their own clients. These actions destroyed any rational boundary and caused the behavior of the United States to lapse into foolishness and crime.

The first serious opposition to U.S. military intervention in Indochina after Kennedy took office was offered by Ernest Gruening of Alaska and Wayne Morse of Oregon. Morse's concern was a double one. Not only did he view this activity as imperialism without foundation on U.S. interest, but he saw the intervention as the final unraveling of constitutional niceties including the right of the Congress to declare war. Morse understood better than Kennedy or McNamara that even the national security state needed a legitimizing frame for its actions. Once the decision was made during the Kennedy period to avoid constitutional niceties, the state's legitimacy was greatly undermined. It appeared that national security matters and the right of the men of the state to act superseded the constitutional frame. In the most profound sense, the Cuban Missile Crisis represented another exercise in delegitimization just because the life of every citizen and of everyone else was risked, and citizenship was no more than what a president's men decided it was worth when they would threaten war.

It is usually taken for granted that the greatest

success of Kennedy's administration was the 1962
Cuban Missile Crisis. There is however, another in-
terpretation. The U.S. military concluded that the
Soviets would stay in their own sphere of influence in
Eastern Europe because they were faced down in
Cuba. This emboldened the United States to assume
that the Soviets had no interest in the North Vietnamese and therefore encouraged the United States
to move into Indochina in force. The Cuban Missile
Crisis allowed U.S. military leadership to deceive
themselves about their own invincibility, especially
against the wretched in the third world. As wrong as
they were, their calculations were less mistaken than
those of militarized civilians like Harold Brown and
Robert McNamara. They constantly underestimated
the Vietnamese and believed strongly in the technology of organization and the organizations of technology as the primary means to dominate situations and
the future. The U.S. military and national security
leaders and planners have acquired mixed attitudes
as a result of the Indochina War. Military planners
believe that force should be used quickly in an overwhelming fashion and without the principles of esca-
lation which were so popular during the late 1950s
and 1960s. Military planners believe that the United
States must eschew a drawn out war because the body
politic in the United States is fragile and isolationist,
and its civilian leaders are fickle. This line of thinking results in greater reliance on deputies who pursue the bidding of U.S. policy, a large-scale arms sale
and loan system that is tightly managed, and a commitment to the use of nuclear weapons when the
situation deteriorates. The willingness to use nuclear
weapons is intended to scare off other great powers
from involvement.

Another group within the national security bureaucracy, especially those brought to authority by President Carter, seeks to avoid direct military involvement unless there is a demonstrable basis that the interests of the United States are involved. Obligations to Israel, sometimes to Korea, and often to NATO are given as examples of such interests. This list also includes oil supplies to the United States.

It should be noted that sublimited wars and limited war preparations, even though they are costly and forge an interdependent corporate system with the state as well as an imperial stance in the world, are of secondary importance to the national security state. Its real foundation is the nuclear weapon and missile. These weapons defined the need for secrecy and the potentiality of world hegemony and influence. So-called rational nuclear strategists view these weapons as "the club in the closet." This club, however, whose existence shaped the nature of the post-World War II state has held the world in fear and awe. Ironically, U.S. leaders do not know if the weapons should be employed in battle or only for political threat purposes, and U.S. generals now candidly admit that the United States has run out of targets. Nevertheless, the arms and acquisition process continues because of the millions of people who are now committed in their humdrum way to the existence of this mode of genocidal war, attack or defense.

During the transition period, President Ford's Department of Defense prepared some briefings and issue papers for Carter and Brown which details the U.S. interest in nuclear weapons as an instrument of war and deterrence. I am including a section of one of these papers on the theory of deterrence and first strike, prepared by the director of Defense Research and Engineering because it illustrates so well the official one-dimensional view of people, states, resources, and psychology which has so defined the thinking of the national security state.

Briefing Paper[1]

Purpose: To describe weapons systems under development which might be:
—Construed as having a first strike capability
—Subjects of concern in arms control negotiations because of:

    —Possible verification on problems.
    —Possible threats to Soviet strategic war-making capabilities.

1. *Possible First Strike Weapons*

The only conceivable reason for our attempting a first strike would be to disarm the Soviets, i.e., to deliver a surprise initial attack of such magnitude as to reduce to a relatively negligible level the Soviet capacity for retaliation. Otherwise, we invite their retaliation. They have an assured second strike capability—achieved through a TRIAD similar to our own—which we cannot obliterate by any present or proposed capability, or even by capabilities which are still in the realm of speculation. At least twice in the last thirty years the Soviets did *not* have an assured retaliatory capability; they were engaged in provoking us; and yet, it was not in our nature to attempt even limited military action against them.

The ability to execute a disarming first strike requires three essentials:
    —Accurate location of *all* Soviet strategic weapons.
    —Sufficient weapons to attack effectively *all* Soviet strategic weapons.
    —Surprise.

We do not possess either of the first two military capabilities and our open society forecloses the third essential. Still, there are some who believe that the development of certain weapons systems poses a potential first strike capability. In this context, a hard target kill (HTK) capability is most often cited as a first strike capability. An HTK capability would be necessary but not sufficient, without satisfying the above criteria, for a first strike. U.S. HTK capabilities and goals derive from a desire for effectiveness and efficiency in a retaliatory role, and—for those weapons targeted against his strategic nuclear forces—to destroy his residual or reserve force to preclude coercion or further war-making capacity after the event of hostilities.

Not only do we not seek a first strike capability, we seek to reduce incentives for an opponent to strike first in a crisis situation by providing our forces with such characteristics that an aggressor would not significantly change the outcome by striking first in a crisis. This is the essence of strategic stability.

Those systems most frequently criticized as having a first strike capability are:

    a. M-X.

[Deleted]

. . .which will be deceptively based among a large number of hardened aim points. It will satisfy requirements for, [1] multiple aim point basing to redress the increasing vulnerability of silo based ICBM's; [2] greater payload to somewhat offset the existing Soviet throw-weight advantage in new ICBM's and SLBM's; and, [3] the capability to attack effectively an expanded and harder set of targets.

Through M-X development we seek the ability to maintain a credible second strike which is in fact that which deters a Soviet first strike. However, the ultimate foundation of the credible second strike is in numbers of deployed weapons and *not* in the weapon system development. They are separable considerations.

M-X multiple aim point basing is criticized by some on the grounds that it is difficult to verify numbers of missiles. We note that while this may be true in the general case, deployment constraints can be devised which permit high confidence counting even without on-site inspection, and that on-site counting is quite reliable, in any event. Banning mobile missiles is tantamount to giving up on ICBM's, since it is only a matter of time before the survivability of U.S. silo-based ICBM's will be unacceptably low. Further, mobile ICBM's, because of their high survivability, do not invite a first strike (there is no premium for striking first) and hence represent a stabilizing influence.

b. Improved Yield and Accuracy for MINUTEMAN. MINUTEMAN III is being improved

[Deleted]

...These are interim improvements to redress throw-weight asymmetries and maintain essential equivalence pending the availability of M-X. Numbers of MINUTEMAN III are inadequate, even with improved accuracy and higher yield, to represent a first strike threat.

c. MaRV (Maneuvering Reentry Vehicle)

MaRV's are potentially applicable to any ballistic missile. They have two applications. One is for evading defensive missiles, the other is for improving overall missile system accuracy.

[Deleted]

As with other weapons systems or components, this development does not threaten any adversary. Further, deployed quantities can satisfy, potentially only one of the three essential criteria for a first strike.

d. Bombers and Cruise Missiles.

These represent no conceivable first strike potential because of the long flight times involved.

2. *Subjects of Concern—Verification*

    a. M-X: Discussed above under first strike.

    b. Cruise Missiles: Two cruise missiles are currently in advanced development: the air launched cruise missile (ALCM) and the TOMAHAWK sea launched cruise missile. The ALCM, deployed on B-52s, could significantly enhance bomber force effectiveness by diluting Soviet air defenses, supplementing penetration range, and providing increased overall targeting flexibility. There are two versions of the TOMAHAWK. The conventionally armed anti-ship TOMAHAWK will provide the Navy a much needed capability to insure that our ships and submarines will not be out-ranged by potential adversaries. The nuclear armed Land Attack TOMAHAWK could be deployed on submarines, surface ships, aircraft, and mobile land launchers for tactical or strategic attack.

Both ALCM and TOMAHAWK are highly accurate, flexible, inexpensive weapons. They are small, aerodynamic vehicles that fly at high subsonic speeds at very low altitude making them very difficult to detect and destroy. They use TERCOM terrain matching guidance, system turbine engine, nuclear warhead. It is expected that a decision will be made in the next few months on whether to enter engineering development with either ALCM or TOMAHAWK or both.

If cruise missiles are covered in future SAL agreements, there could be two aspects of compliance verification to be addressed. The first aspect could be verification of the total number of cruise missiles deployed or in storage and the second could involve limits on range of the missiles.

[Deleted]

There is no known adequate technical basis for verifiably constraining cruise missile range. For example, some current Soviet missiles, with substantially less range than the potential U.S. cruise missiles, are physically much larger than the U.S. cruise missiles would be. An overriding consideration bearing on the problem of limiting cruise missile range is the fact that the geographical distribution of Soviet targets requires a long range for U.S. cruise missiles whereas heavy coastal population and industrial concentration in the United States permits attack by short range Soviet cruise missiles. There is no realistic way to differentiate between tactical and strategic cruise missiles.

3. *Subject of Concern—Threats to Soviet Strategic War-Making Capabilities*

    a. U.S. Offensive Systems: Discussed in 1. above.

    b. ABM: We have no deployed ABM capability. We have a program ($200M) in advanced component and systems technology. No weapons system is under development. ABM RED has the following objectives which represent no threat to any Soviet strategic war-making capability:

      —Maintain a capability to develop and deploy an ABM system should one be required for defense of ICBM forces, C^3 systems, or other high value targets.

      —Maintain the U.S. lead in ABM technology through investigation of advanced components, technologies, and systems concepts that could yield a technological breakthrough.

    c. Space Defense:

[Deleted]

I have introduced this transition document to show why the nature of war preparation should come under legal scrutiny. There is little doubt that the security of the people, and therefore, human rights, are directly violated by the nature of weaponry which a state procures. In modern states, huge organizations enter into a series of activities on a daily basis that may not appear to be crimes or violations of anyone's rights due to their abstracted or humdrum nature. Who would think, having read the plans of Eichmann for the use of railway trains, that he was involved in genocide? But in reality, once we are able to remove the conceptual blinders from our eyes, we see that those humdrum actions are crimes. The armaments race, given the nature of the arms made and the war plans fashioned, is criminal in nature when compared to laws of war or peace, the criminal laws of individual nations, and the Nuremberg and Asian trial standards. The nuclear armaments system seems to fall within the framework of the first four articles of the Nuremberg Charter. Thus, the arms strategists' plans for "taking out" millions of people either in first or second strike reprisal are surely not contemplated by any internationally lawful system of defense. That we see nations and their leaders thoughtlessly reducing their actions to criminal activity hardly means that laws do not exist which directly contradict such behavior. As the judges at Nuremberg said, " ... after the policy to initiate and wage aggressive wars was formulated, if a defendant came into possession of knowledge that the invasions and war to be waged were aggressive and unlawful (against international law and treaty), then he will be criminally responsible if he, being on the policy level, could have influenced such policy and failed to do so." [2] Thus, since such actions once contemplated are war crimes *in situ* due to their genocidal or illegal nature, we are faced with a complicated conceptual problem. The final frame or act in a process which leads to a culminating event (in this case, the go signal for nuclear war) does not have to be completed for us to realize that the event is already underway. One needs only to look at arms budgets and strategic doctrine to comprehend the criminal nature of the arms enterprise.

The development of scientific and technological wizardry in relation to the ability of a bureaucracy to organize the resources of the society for military and defense purposes has resulted in armaments becoming the measure of state power. As the armaments race deepens, the moral contradiction of it becomes more obvious. This moral contradiction is also reflected in the fact that the armaments themselves increase anxiety, distort the value and priority structure within the arming nation, and ultimately cause an inter-dependent link between military bureaucracies of opposing sides who use each other to rationalize their commitment to arming.

It is not too late to break this dance of death. In this context, the following three questions should be considered: (1) If the United States were now to stop any further production of nuclear weapons and missiles, would it be any less secure? (2) Should not U.S. government officials be held to standards of personal accountability, as outlined in Kastenmeier's proposed bill,[3] so that aggressive war will not be a part of the national security bureaucrat's kit? (3) Should people in the armed forces be able to unionize for wages, hours, and a code of ethics which would exclude the use of genocidal weapons and participation in aggressive wars? In other words, should soldiers and sailors have the power to limit the mode of weaponry and destruction by abiding by an oath of conduct that eschews such weaponry and acts as a control over unconstitutional wars of aggression?

While such questions must now be opened and debated in society as a whole, it is still necessary to press for disarmament arrangements through the national security bureaucracies as they are presently organized. In 1961 the United States and the Soviet Union agreed to the McCloy-Zorin Eight Points which outlined principles for obtaining universal disarmament.[4] This memorandum could be used as a basis for reopening the disarmament question. In 1963 the signatories to the partial Test Ban Treaty proclaimed as their principal aim "the speediest possible achievement of an agreement on general and complete disarmament under strict international control in accordance with the objectives of the United Nations which would put an end to the armaments race and eliminate the incentive to the production and testing of all kinds of weapons, including nuclear weapons."[5]

It is possible to set the motion for general disarmament in three stages. As a first stage, the United States must undertake unilateral steps such as banning future missile production as well as uranium and plutonium production. Outmoded alliance commitments which justify elaborate military forces must be transformed. A process of agonizing reappraisal and reconsideration must be instituted in the bureaucracy so that policy decisions for disarmament will not be sabotaged.

This will make possible a second stage which will include the disarmament of troops, nuclear weapons, and missiles from different regions of the world. Thus, for example, the concept of the nuclear-free zone should be reinitiated for the Pacific. The context for discussion on disarmament in the second stage could begin in the United Nations Security Council with the permanent members laying out the basis for determining the questions and concerns of disarmament. The United States, for example, should convene a United Nations Security Council meeting with a series of studies about disarmament, including the means of accomplishing and preserving it. These disarmament proposals would be debated in the council for at least a year during which time a position upon which there was agreement could develop. That position would include the following steps: consensus on what nations should do without inspection; the reduction of missiles and nuclear weapons, unilaterally and through negotiation; development of inspection techniques and collateral forms of inspection; budget examinations as suggested under the Helsinki agreements; and the reduction and abolition of armaments over a period of ten years. In the past, plans have correctly called for the staged reduction of armaments in which the great powers would reduce their forces first in the context of a worldwide disarmament and arms control plan. Less heavily armed nations would be more likely to follow suit.

In a third stage, the success of so-called confidence building measures would cause national leaders to move toward the abolition of weapons and armed forces. Such plans should now be exhumed and studied in the light of current needs and realities. It should be noted that certain new plans have been proposed which bear careful study as they include the actions of nongovernmental groups and citizens.

The Defense Department budget increases for the 1978-85 period are projected to reach $250 billion by 1985.[6] It is to be expected that the Soviet defense budget and those of other nations will correspondingly increase. Because no security or budgetary relief is in sight, our choices are stark and obvious.

The dialectical hope that arming for war will prevent it or the shamanistic belief in the one-dimensional psychological assumption that arming with nuclear weapons and missiles will scare other parties in the arms race as long as the leadership believes it is either ahead or needs to catch up does not recognize a more central reality. This reality is that the use of this weaponry and preparation for its use is part of a continuum that shades policy into crime and guarantees criminal behavior. Government officials descend to the level of bureaucratic gangsterism as their political lives and practices fly directly in the face of Article One of the Charter and the Declaration of Human Rights.

Throughout the cold war, congressional luminaries such as Senators Stennis and Eastland of Mississippi, Senator Dodd of Connecticut, Senator Russell and Congressman Vinson of Georgia, and Pennsylvania Congressman Walter praised such behavior and operated as the bulldogs that guarded the anticommunist and imperial writ of the national security state. Their rhetoric and the covenant of imperialism neatly masked the problem of nuclear war. They successfully stopped the peace movement except in the case of nuclear testing in the atmosphere in which poisoning from fallout could not be denied. But this victory was a limited one. Some, like Leo Szilard, raised questions about the test ban agreement, saying that it would increase rather than decrease nuclear testing and therefore quicken the pace of the arms race. He correctly believed that it would not result in one less weapon being designed or acquired. Underground testing increased threefold during this period, and the arms race continued at essentially the same pace.[7] Once the atmospheric test ban was achieved, the peace movement lost interest in the arms race. It moved to a different problem, and its success was undeniable.

There were different stages in the antiwar movement related to the state of the arms race. In the 1950s peace groups were seized by the problem of nuclear weapons and atomic testing. These questions were usually viewed as being of a technical nature or as products of one's pacifist beliefs. The middle class registered its concern through SANE and magazines such as the *Saturday Review*. Criticism of the arms race was a means of being political without being un-American.

There was wide support from 1955 to 1963 for a test ban agreement, but it remained the concern of people in the middle class. Parenthetically, the poor and working class have not concerned themselves with nuclear disarmament. There are several reasons for this not readily recognized by those who do not work in factories. The first is that most industrial workers find that factory conditions are similar to chemical warfare, but it is waged against them. Very few people outside the factory care about disarmament within the factory. Secondly, the jobs of workers have become intertwined with the arms race and neither major political party has been prepared to support an alternative which would guarantee income security of the worker so he could exercise choice about working in armaments. Scientific workers, of course, rose in status and security with the arms race.

The members of the middle class did not see the empire or their ambiguous position in it. The educational system should take much credit for their blindness. Liberal teaching was not prepared to analyze imperialism or call things by their right names. Instead, as Ann Wilcox pointed out, imperialist values were internalized and seen as necessary to create consensus. In the 1950s when the Soviets said the Rockefellers had great power in the United States, students and professors would laugh uproariously at the simplistic Soviet propaganda. All Soviet views of the United States were used in schools as evidence of ideological paranoia and craziness of the vulgar Soviet propagandists. C. Wright Mills was an outcast among social scientists because he said there was a power elite in the United States. Although middle class academics and the media refused to accept the idea of the ruling class, members of it had no such reluctance.

The ruling belief system was challenged seriously only by the black community during this period. Black people were far more aware of the power structure of life in the United States than the white middle class which was insulated by the appearance of options and opportunities. Yet there were some quizzical voices.

When Krushchev came to the United States in 1960, he asked to meet with the ruling class, and everyone laughed about it. I have spoken with several people who were present at the 1960 meeting. They said it was not a funny meeting at all and that Khrushchev was correct in courting them. Carter's cabinet should dispel all illusions on the importance of the Rockefeller family. The middle class and the working class in the 1950s, however, believed there was no ruling class. There was no organized leftist party in the United States to suggest otherwise since it was thrown out of all major institutions. The ruling belief system was challenged seriously only by the black community during 1940-50 period. Black people were far more aware of the power structure of life in the United States than the white middle class which was insulated by the appearance of options and opportunities.

In certain universities from 1949-61, a type of dissent existed which borrowed from Fabianism notions of incrementalism. Quakers including Stewart Meacham and the sociologist David Riesman sought to keep the Fabian flame burning. The Communist Party was decimated and infiltrated. To the extent it held together, it was done so by agents and informers of the FBI. However, the Left, as it had been understood prior to 1948, was nonexistent except in the aspirations of the civil rights movement and of the very few Quakers and nonviolent resisters in the peace movement including Dorothy Day, A.J. Muste, and Paul Goodman. The more important people's movement revolved around civil rights in Alabama under black leadership which cracked the internal colonizing hegemony. While the peace movement was a little thorn in the side of the government, the rights of black people reached to the very fundamentals of the constitutional system of the United States. Eisenhower found that he had no choice but to back up the Supreme Court which legitimated the struggle of the civil rights movement in *Brown* v. *Board of Education of Topeka*.[13]

Attorney General William Rogers in Eisenhower's administration, believed that the Supreme Court had to be sustained for reasons of upholding authority. Eisenhower, raised in a border state, attempted to undercut the court by saying that desegregation could not be brought about by legal means; it could only occur through better community relations and education. Once Eisenhower took the position that understanding would only come through education, he was caught in a bind. If education were the chosen instrument to solve the racial conflict in the United States, it was necessary to desegregate the schools.

Desegregation became an important issue for another reason: to blacks, desegregation meant citizenship. But to the national state it meant propaganda for imperial aspiration. The submissions to the Supreme Court in *Brown* v. *Board of Education of Topeka* included a brief from Dean Acheson who argued that the United States had to desegregate because it needed to show the rest of the world that it was not racist—a charge that was often made by the Soviet Union. In addition, the State Department argued that there was a contradiction between the United States presenting itself as the world's greatest democracy and leader of the free world while blacks were denied basic rights. A few years before in 1948, the NAACP sent the United Nations Security Council and the General Assembly an appeal for help on the issue of segregation.[9] This was a source of great embarrassment for the United States. Liberal elements within the national security state favored a desegregation program that was consistent with the propaganda developed by the USIA and the CIA since an internal desegregation program strengthened the propaganda hand of the United States in the so-called underdeveloped nations. Propaganda was judged an important part of the cold war. From 1948 to 1953 the Smith-Mundt Act "tripled the size of the overseas information program."

It is important to note that the national security managers were not racist in the way that fascists were racist. While they unconsciously embraced the cult of the blood in that they believed in the superiority of western civilization, its science, technology, and common law, they had imbibed enough of twentieth century democratic rhetoric to know that racism was not a basis for the efficient operations of the state. Corporate firms including space contractors argued that business expansion was held back by local customs of segregation and racism. Such conventions interfered with the market place, industrial production, and scientific sensibilities.

Most scientists dependent on government grants for research played a complicated insider-outsider game. They willingly placed their graduate students in military research, gave advice to the governments for the construction of weaponry, signed petitions in their scientific organizations against them, and participated in conferences such as Pugwash, in hopes of getting the Soviets to accept their view of the arms race. These conferences became increasingly conservative in tone as government strategists and weapons scientists began participating in them. Scientists rationalized their ambiguous activities by arguing for the importance of countering negative forces within the government that sought nuclear war or more weaponry. Thus, the President's Science Advisory Committee (PSAC) rationalized its role in this way. Its members, and their scientific/academic colleagues favored government subsidy for their "good" experiments in exchange for a touch of defense consulting.

In the 1960s university students resented the role of their professors and the types of grants and contracts which the various national security agencies dangled before universities. White middle class students who had gone to Mississippi returned to their own campuses and raised the issue of students rights and the way in which their universities were used. By

1965 student discontent focused on the Indochina War. Black activists, following the lead of Martin Luther King, Jr., and SNCC, began demonstrating against the war in the spring of 1965. Also, in that year the teach-in movement, which began at the University of Michigan and the University of Wisconsin, spread to all campuses including government agencies. The purposes were of an informational nature. Professors and students believed that those who were against the war should be able to debate with policy workers in the national security state and the military with facts. It started in a rather precise and defensive way. A number of the war's opponents believed that since U.S. leaders were rational men who believed in facts, they would have no choice but to give up the imperial war. Indeed, *The Vietnam Reader*, the book which I wrote with Bernard Fall, has a bit of that quality to it. We agreed with academics that if we got out all the facts, people would be able to recognize and choose the right side. Our optimism even extended to bureaucrats whom we believed were also ignorant of the facts. While there was something childish and naive about this point of view, some people had their political consciousness changed by this approach.

Within two years, the government bureaucrats who used to come around and debate on the various campuses stopped doing so because there was nothing they could say. The campuses became violent on the issue. It was hard for administration spokesmen to speak at universities. There was one extraordinary incident in 1967 in which McNamara ran through the basements of various Harvard tunnels to get away from a posse of students.

In 1967-68 a part of the antiwar movement turned

to resistance. In black communities, many black college students refused to go to war. They kicked in store windows courting felony charges against them for destruction of property so they would escape the draft. Others in the South undertook to stand trial for resistance, and they invariably got the longest sentences. SNCC people who took on the draft resistance issue in the South ended up getting ten-year sentences.

In the East from 1965 to 1967, the antiwar marches began in Washington and culminated in the Pentagon March in which McNamara's own children marched against the Pentagon. There is a terrifying picture of McNamara looking at the crowd in silhouette. He resembled a Spanish cardinal of the Inquisition looking at a mob. The mob brought fear to the government officials, and the roles of the informant and the police increased greatly so that public order could be restored. In the first fifteen years of the national security state, national police actions by the military outside of the United States from Korea to Guatemala were followed by police actions against cities in the United States and their populaces. Before 1960 movements to reform the police came from business interests and social scientists who saw police reform as a part of social engineering. The police were thought to be crucial in bringing about a standard of behavior which could be successfully enforced on the poor and the workers. Throughout the twentieth century, the purpose of police reform has been to bring about new scientific techniques, and to better educate police and to play down police violence. Their community relations task was to develop a system of loyalty which the poor and the alienated could embrace. Reformers sought greater coordination among the local police and less dependence on local communities. In other words, they hoped to build up a responsive police structure nationally. These ideas were first spelled out by the Wickersham Commission of 1931. They did not, however, receive general acceptance among the elites until the civil rights and antiwar struggles of the 1960s. By 1966 the national security state found that it could no longer take a relaxed and relatively detached attitude toward the civil society. It was critical to develop a system which made clear that crime, as understood by the better elements of the society, had to be stopped. The Justice Department and Congress feared simultaneous uprisings in the major cities which would require the use of tens of thousands of combat troops. Federal officials did not have confidence in local police forces or the locally controlled intelligence operations in the event of such uprisings.

The social turbulence during 1966-71 caused the business classes and professional reformers to seek varying modes of internal pacification. There were two schools of thought on this question. One view, held by Morris Janowitz, was that the operations of the National Guard caused the spread of violence. It did not appear to act in a just manner, and consequently, its actions stimulated greater anger and revolt.[10] Unsoldierly and unpolicemanlike conduct was criticized by the liberals who believed that if the police and the armed forces could be made more professional, excesses would not occur. This point of view was also held by the liberal Attorney General Ramsey Clark.[11] But in addition to professionalizing the state coercive apparatus, there were widespread moves initiated by the liberals to infiltrate the ghettos through the use of informers. One such program was supervised by John Doar, another liberal assistant attorney general who later served as the House Judiciary Committee's special counsel on the impeachment of Richard Nixon. Files were established about people that could serve as a police grid to find dissidents. Of course, various agencies such as the FBI had long used *agents provocateurs* as a standard operating procedure.

Large business and private complexes also expanded their private police forces. These are not, however, private armies in the sense that they once existed in Italy or in western United States. Nevertheless, they are widespread and significant. Their political influence is unknown and not thought about. There is an association of retired FBI agents which operates in part as an "old boy" network. Many former agents direct security and private police force operations for corporations. Allied with this group is a network of CIA agents that operates through proprietaries, international business, law firms, and former intelligence agents who sell their services to the CIA on contract.

As one might have expected, the strategies for maintaining order in the third world were reintroduced in cities in the United States. Military contractors such as North American Aviation, Hughes Aircraft, and IBM actively sought government contracts for developing police technology, computer systems, and social models for controlling social unrest. The LEAA, Law Enforcement Assistance Administration, saw itself as an instrument to modernize all the police forces in the United States and to develop new command and control systems, communications systems (sophisticated technology as it was called), and gathering of suspects through the National

Crime Information Center (NCIC) which handles about 130,000 transactions a day. It should be remembered that one out of every three adults in the United States has a criminal arrest record (around 50 million people). In 1974 the public expenditures for criminal justice totaled 14 billion dollars, 8 billion went for the police. There is a set of a symbolic examples which shows that the imperial mindset is not bounded by territorial limits. Cyrus Vance and Warren Christopher, Carter's secretary and undersecretary of state, worked together during the Johnson administration in putting down black rebellions in the United States and setting up a surveillance system in the cities. John McCone, a former director of the CIA, headed the California commission on the Watts Riots.

The fear which the federal government had of street demonstrations during 1966-70 was far greater than anyone on the streets realized at the time. There were thousands of people who went to jail as easily as they would light up a joint or drink a cocktail. By so doing, they were announcing their allegiance to America as the civil society and their contempt of state power. This stage of the peace movement was reached when it became clear through television and reports which filtered back from soldiers that the war was a criminal fraud. Members of Congress said that one-fourth of the South Vietnamese Army was run by the National Liberation Front, that the refugee problem was horrendous, and that Saigon itself was like Shanghai during 1948-49. It had become the seventh circle of hell. Soldiers returned saying that the war was putrid and the only thing the Americans were getting from it was drug addiction and clap. It is no wonder that people began to doubt the leadership of the country and that most Americans did not believe official versions of the way things operate.

Describing this phenomenon in *Being and Doing*, I tried to look beyond the question of healthy doubt which people have of official explanations.[12] When people believe that what they do has no relationship to what they feel, they are likely to doubt objective explanations of behaviors. They know that such behaviors, while others may describe them as objective reality, do not deal with affective feeling which is not recognized because it is not expressed. Consequently, many matches can light the fire of discontent concealed by objectivity, and the objective observer is always surprised. A few years ago, there was an empirical study of a plant in Great Britain. The social scientists concluded that on the basis of what they thought they saw, the workers were contented. Publication of this study resulted in a wildcat strike which showed the actual feelings of the workers.

Maccoby and Riesman commented in 1962 that several years before there was a generalized belief that Negro colleges, as they were then called, were sleepy places with no concern for civil rights.[13] But several years later, it proved that the exact opposite was true once the dry leaves were ignited by those who allowed their subjective sensibility to break through the reality which was created for them. This matter, however, is somewhat beyond our subject.

In 1968 the authority of political institutions and the beliefs which supported them were under attack on a world-wide scale. The state appeared to have little support outside of itself. The Department of Justice failed to sustain its position in important conspiracy trials against the antiwar resistance. An

almost successful student-led social revolution in
France brought down de Gaulle. The unsuccessful
Czech revolution revealed the Soviet Union once and
for all as a conservative status quo power in Eastern
Europe as it sent Asian Soviet troops to put down the
Czechoslovak grasp at liberation. The cultural revolution in China sought to break the bureaucracy of
the state. And after the Tet offensive in 1968, the U.S.
military was left with the choice of invading North
Vietnam, using nuclear weapons, or leaving because
it had lost the support of its own people. In that year,
the Catholic Church also faced the dissolution of its
ecclesiastical authority on major questions of faith
and secular life.[14]

During 1969-71 U.S. international corporations
such as American Express, Chase Bank, and United
Fruit were bombed in Latin America, Europe, and
Asia. The war was not a free ride for business and
corporate leaders such as the chairman of the Bank of
America who testified against the Vietnam War before the Senate Foreign Relations Committee. With
Clark Clifford's turnabout in 1968 on the Indochina
War, capitalism in the United States sought a way to
cut its losses in Indochina. As Truman's counsel, Clifford had been a leading cold warrior who suggested
the use of atomic and bacteriological weapons against
the Soviet Union in an important memorandum to
President Truman. This memorandum, a composite
view of the members of Truman's cabinet, set the
terms of the cold war and of the arms race. When
Clifford became secretary of defense, he confronted
Johnson with the fact that he had lost the support of
the business community.[15] The loss of business support together with the effect of the antiwar movement
forced Johnson to resign. Of course, forcing Johnson
out did not mean that the great corporations were no

longer imperial. They recognized their interests more precisely and concluded that the cost of the war exceeded the price. Schumpeter had long ago spoken of the capitalist antipathy to war in modern social life, and his insight was not betrayed by the great corporations.[16] The great capitalists said no, but the war continued another six years. Once the contracts were set, careers committed, projections made, and the bureaucratic interests established, ending such a war would necessarily take years. It is a mistake to say that the United States let the war be lost. At least 2.5 million U.S. troops served in Vietnam over a seven-year period. For purposes of comparison, the reader should note that at the height of the French occupation and war in Indochina, the French fielded an armed force of no more than 220,000 troops. The U.S. Air Force bombed Indochina with three times as much of the entire bomb tonnage used in World War II. The bombing policies were from their inception state terror tactics meant to break Hanoi's will. Later other reasons were added: bombing was a way to keep the support of the hawks in Congress and of the various South Vietnamese governments which U.S. officials made and broke with impunity. It was cynically rationalized as a way to keep the faith with American prisoners of war.

One should not forget the decision made by Nixon and Kissinger to order massive bombings of Hanoi and Haiphong. It would be well to quote from the account of the Vietnam Worker's Party on the bombing and the losses to see how intense the air struggle had become by 1972 during the so-called phasing out period.

Over a period of twelve days—December 18-19, 1972—

the U.S. imperialists dropped 100,000 tons of bombs (40,000 tons on Hanoi), the equivalent of five atomic bombs of the kind dropped on Hiroshima in 1945 . . . . The North Vietnamese shot down 81 U.S. planes among them 34 B52s and 5 F111s. Hanoi alone brought down 30 aircraft, among them 23 B52s and 2 F111s. During the second U.S. war of destruction—from April to December 1972—the armed force and people of the North had shot down nearly 700 U.S. aircraft including 54 B52s and 10 F111s and had sunk and set afire many U.S. war vessels.[17]

The United States, which began the war as South Vietnam's advisors, ended with having the South Vietnamese as their advisors. Mao Tse-tung predicted this course of the war in 1962-63 in conversations with western journalists including Edgar Snow.[18]

U.S. leaders differed in military strategies, but they were prepared to test all of them simultaneously and in the process visit great brutality on the Vietnamese people. One was the so-called enclave strategy which called for holding Saigon and the coastal cities of Nhu Trang and Qui Nbon. Another strategy was a war of attrition which would be tied to search and destroy tactics. It was a traditional army strategy aimed at destroying the enemy wherever the enemy could be found. The problem with this strategy which guided the U.S. war on the ground was that the South Vietnamese people ended up being the enemy, and the war of attrition was fought against the entire people. Experts believed that in order to have carried out such a war, it would have taken ten American soldiers to defeat one NLF or North Vietnamese soldier since a substantial portion of the South Vietnamese people supported and were part of the NLF.

The United States would have been required to field an armed force of some 6 million men to make this strategy successful. Needless to say, such a force would have meant placing the United States on a war footing requiring a declaration of war and a higher objective equal to the commitment of so many young men. Rusk and Eugene Rostow courted a war with China in the hopes of finding meaning to the Asian adventure. This political move would have increased the likelihood of even greater turbulence within the United States. After Tet in January 1968, the United States changed its search and destroy policy to a more defensive strategy of turning the war back to the Vietnamese. Johnson's political weakness in his own party aborted a more aggressive military strategy. There was also military weakness in the field.

As David Cortright has shown in his book *Soldiers in Revolt*, it was one thing for military leaders to have a military strategy, and it was quite another to get the average American soldier to go along with either the war or the strategies. In 1971-72 numerous U.S. troops and units refused to fight, and the South Vietnamese armed forces were in a virtual state of collapse. There was evidence of this situation in 1968 as U.S. military leaders debated whether to have a land invasion of North Vietnam, use nuclear weapons, or begin the process of withdrawal. It was the strength of the antiwar forces in the United States, the protest marches, the campus turbulence, and the rather surprising success of the Gene McCarthy movement which stopped the invasion of North Vietnam in March 1968. The policy makers were faced with a dilemma. Should they begin a slow withdrawal from Indochina or use tactical nuclear weapons for its ambiguous objectives? The second choice was rejected because it put the United States into a position of using nuclear weapons for purposes that were absolutely unclear. There was, however, a hidden reason. The children and wives of the ruling leadership would have deserted the leaders. While the leaders would have scared everybody literally to death in other parts of the world, they would also have caused great political disruption within the United States itself without accomplishing any particular military objective in Vietnam. What was the point? The Joint Chiefs of Staff had considered the question of using nuclear weapons in similar circumstances during the Korean War. But according to Omar Bradley, the chairman of the Joint Chiefs, the military could not find a suitable target.

Imperial forces should never be overestimated. Even if a military victory is won by imperial forces, as the French did in Algeria, it doesn't mean that those who wear the imperial mantle have won a political victory. They are not able to forge a military victory into political economic stability or gain support from the people. In 1972 I talked with the NLF and the North Vietnamese representatives in Paris. It was a very instructive exchange for me. It was the spring of 1972, and the North Vietnamese had begun a spring offensive in the highlands. Ambassador Vy asked me what the official reaction of the United States would be. I said, "In the next year, the United States will respond by bombing the dikes."

"And then?"

"Then the military will mine the harbors of Haiphong."
"And then?"

"Then the United States will try to destroy
Hanoi through air bombing."
"And then?"
"Then the military will recommend bombing
Saigon."
"And then?"

The civil society of the United States, the people
within the various institutions, already understood
the Vietnamese point and were making their will
known in no uncertain terms. At a national security
council meeting in 1967, General Westmoreland
suggested that the president put three-quarters of a
million and then a million troops into Vietnam.
Johnson fled the meeting saying that Westmoreland
must be crazy. Johnson thought that the demonstrators would scale the fences, jump over, and
occupy the White House. Johnson understood what
those insulated by the bureaucracy and military life
did not understand. It was that the national security
state had not yet engulfed the entire civil society.
While the state attempts to blanket the entire civil
society, it finds resistance. When it is caught out in
war, it has to find a way of increasing its own legitimacy, and the only way that it can do so is if it sells
the people a *raison d'etre* for war or finds other purposes. During the Korean expedition, a *raison d'etre*
was found using the U.N. and anticommunism as its
legitimating instrument. Even the Korean War was
not swallowed whole. Taft conservatives believed
that war to be unnecessary and unconstitutional.

While the imperial objective of militarily holding
onto southeast Asia has been lost, it is absurd to think
that the national security state apparatus can disap-
pear. The apparatus searches for a place to fix its

energies and prove its need. The national security state's existence is predicated on a series of objectives which are both external (in terms of having an interest or supporting interests which particular elites, bureaucrats, the military, planners, and corporations fashion around the world) and internal (the ability to keep the economic structure flowing so that interclass stability is maintained).

For example, Kissinger's form of detente was intended to produce new markets for a number of corporations which could set up banks and traders in hitherto forbidden territories. Joint operating arrangements between multinational corporations and socialist countries meant that the methods of imperialism, and, therefore, the assumptions of an anticommunist bureaucracy would have to change. Furthermore, according to some planners of the State Department, once the Indochina War ended and great power detente was achieved, guerrilla movements in third world countries would not be supported by socialist nations. In addition, the benefits of dealing with the United States would be seen as greater than those dealing with the Soviet Union or a strife-torn China. They could be coopted into the U.S. imperial system on a more businesslike basis. After the end of the Indochina War, the Chinese sought relations with the United States in an effort to obtain support from the United States in their struggle with the Soviet Union. National leaders who don't recognize the primacy of the United States find themselves caught out. There is an interesting example of this point. In 1966 President Marcos of the Philippines spoke to the Congress of the United States and said that it was like coming to the Roman senate during its imperial greatness. The United States directly and indirectly controlled the basic policies of the Philippines. With the American loss in Indochina, the sense of awe among the client states was eroded. A few years later, Marcos went to China; hoping for Mao's blessing before he died, Marcos announced the decline of the influence of the United States in Asia. Soon thereafter Mao died, and China itself was in turmoil and looked for a rapprochment with the United States. Such are the vagaries of international politics. Now Vietnam seeks closer relationships with the U.S. and American corporate investment.

What is neither vague nor changing are certain long-term contradictions which have come to light during times of both war and cold war. The contradiction between the city and the national security state grows greater as it becomes clear to everyone that retaining the imperial conceit and the present defense budgets demands greater and greater sacrifice from the people in the cities, the working and middle classes, especially outside the sunbelt region.

> The Federal government has been milking the civilian parts of the American economy in order to pay for its military enterprise. The crucial evidence is available to us in the form of the taxes paid from the various states to the Federal government, in relation to the payments made into the states by the Federal government. The pattern is unmistakable. The first years for which data are available on this are 1965-1967. In that period the Federal government took out of New York state $7.4 billion more than it spent here for all purposes. By contrast, California received $2 billion a year more than it paid to the Federal government. The surplus in Virginia was $1.3 billion, and for Texas it was $1 billion each year. New York State was not the only one that suffered a major outflow. The other principal states whose wealth was transferred out were Illinois, Michi-

gan, Pennsylvania, Ohio, Indiana, and Wisconsin. The important common feature of all these states is that they are all centers of civilian industry and civilian economy.[19]

There is a growing consciousness in the Northeast that the taxing system of the poor and middle class is a form of theft used to support imperial activity.

And as for the major adversary of the United States? The Soviet Union is itself in the throes of serious cultural, political, and economic problems. The Soviet brand of imperialism and national security concerns cannot point to much as examples of success. The Soviets have held on to frozen definitions of Marxist-Leninism which were taught as unexamined catechism. It has kept up in the arms race through bleeding its own people while pointing to accomplishments in space exploration but precious few on land.

Soviet leaders had started the 1960s with continued denunciations at the Twenty-Second Party Congress of Stalin and the cult of personality. Millions of people had paid a terrible price for Stalin's version of justice. By 1956 Soviet leaders knew that in order to retain any legitimacy with the people, they were required to denounce Stalin and his group. But in their denunciation, the Soviet leaders hastened the loss of the support of China, which used the anti-Stalinist campaign in the Soviet Union as an example of Soviet contempt of revolutionary values. This was a curious turn in Chinese political thinking. The Chinese knew that at every stage Stalin and his group had sought to frustrate independent Chinese development even to the point of having discouraged Chinese communist leadership from making a bid for political power notwithstanding the fact that the

Kuomintang leadership was already broken.

Within the Soviet Union, dissidents such as Roy Medvedyev, who had not rejected the Soviet socialist project as an utter failure, sought to have their views debated in the party and state councils.[20] They adopted the formulation that their plans and schemes could get the Soviet state back on the socialist track. Their criticisms included low economic growth rate, poor and too few consumer goods, misplaced economic priorities, administrative inefficiency, and a deadened body politic which had forgotten how to publicly debate matters in a way that would advance the Soviet nation toward socialist goals. They also embraced technocratic standards of productivity and performance and claimed that the workers were not allowed to produce and work. The claims of Medvedyev and his fellow Samizdat writers were unanswerable as was the fact that Soviet world influence remained secondary to that of the United States and was ambiguous at best even within the socialist realm. The dissidents charged that enough time had elapsed since the terrible destruction which the Soviet people had endured during the Second World War to judge their system in critical Marxist terms.

Internationally, Soviet influence suffered. The split between Chinese and Soviet leadership "turned into estrangement, mutual hostility, and by the end of the 60s, even to open military confrontation, diverting a vast part of the military resources of both countries.[21] Soviet leadership, in its state, party, or ideological role, no longer called the tune among the communists of China, Indochina, Cuba, Italy, or Spain. Within Eastern Europe itself, the national leaderships have chafed under Soviet hegemony. The Soviet performance in Czechoslovakia turned the

Warsaw Pact from a defensive arrangement against NATO into a status quo system to freeze the internal security of the states. The economic imperial position of the Soviets had also slowed integration of the Eastern European nations as a trading bloc. In each area of the world, as for example in the Middle East, the Soviets found themselves playing second fiddle in the international symphony conducted by the United States. Egypt and Syria found the Soviet style operation not to their liking, and other nationalist groupings learned that they had to look to their own cultures and their own people for the type of development which they preferred. No longer would the accidentality of having proclaimed the first socialist revolution mean that the party descendants of that set of revolutionaries would define either the socialist project or the development of national independence. The Left in nonsocialist countries looks suspiciously at communist party members. They are often seen as too bureaucratic and as believing too strongly in centralized authority and "progress." They are thought by some to be a conservative anachronism when it comes to the development of movement and cultural changes. One of the first socialists to understand this situation was R.H.S. Crossman, who said that "more and more serious minded people are having second thoughts about what once seemed to them the obvious advantage of central planning and the extension of State ownership . . . ." Socialism, which came to mean the development of a vast centralized bureaucracy, was a grave danger to democratic socialist principles. Crossman suggested that "the main task of socialists today is to convince the nation that its liberties are threatened by this new feudalism."[22]

The Soviets are in a very difficult national security

bind. Their defense expenditures, which take up a greater portion of their GNP each year, have had the effect of economically depressing the society; their greatest achievements in missile development, however, are mercifully unused. The Soviet state has tied itself, as have our bureaucrats, to an arms race which strangles plans that would change the bellicose purposes of states.

NOTES

1. Director, Defense Research and Engineering, Department of Defense issue paper prepared for 1976-77 transition period.

2. Nuremberg decision, cited in *American Journal of International Law* 41 (1947): pp. 172-333.

3. *Congressional Record* H6396, 8 July 1975 (introduction of *H.R. 8388*, the Official Accountability Act of 1975, by Representative Robert Kastenmeier).

4. Declaration of Disarmament, Department of State Bulletin, 16 October 1976, p. 650.

5. Nuclear Weapons Test Ban, 5 August 1963, 2 U.S.T. 1314, 1316, TIAS No. 5433.

6. Based on $120 billion FY 1978 budget, a straight line projection of 9-11 percent which reflects a 4 percent increase per year in quantum of men and machines for the next three years, plus a 6 percent rate of inflation per year for three years. These are very conservative estimates.

7. Leo Szilard, in conversation with the author.

8. 347 U.S. 483 1954.

9. This document, presented on 23 October 1947, to the Department of Social Affairs of the United Nations carried a long and explicit title: "A Statement on the Denial of Human Rights to Minorities in the Case of Citizens of Negro Descent in the United States of America and an Appeal to the United Nations for Redress Prepared for the National Association for the Advancement of Colored People Under the Editorial Supervision of W.E.B. DuBois, with contributions by Earl B. Dickerson, Milton R. Konvitz, William R. Ming, Leslie S. Perry and Rayford W. Logan."

10. Morris Janowitz, "Social Control and Escalated Riots," in

Violence in America, ed. Tod Gurr and Hugh Graham (New York: Bantam Books, Inc., 1969); also see *The Iron Fist and the Velvet Glove: An Analysis of the U.S. Police*, Center for Research on Criminal Justice (Berkeley, Calif.: 1975), p. 32-37.

11. Ramsey Clark, *Crime in America: Observations on Its Nature, Causes, Prevention and Control* (New York: Simon and Schuster, 1970), pp. 132-88.

12. Marcus Raskin, *Being and Doing*.

13. David Riesman and Michael Maccoby, "The American Crisis," in *The Liberal Papers*, ed. James Roosevelt (Garden City, N.Y.: Doubleday and Co., Inc., 1962), pp. 13-47.

14. I mention the Catholic Church because papal authority between 1943 and 1963 was a crucial stabilizing element in Western Europe. The emergence in Western Europe of a Catholic leadership around Schuman in France, Adenauer in Germany, and De Gasperi in Italy was critical to U.S. plans for Europe. Christian democracy fit perfectly with the framework of the national security state in the United States because it was not to the Left and it coopted the Right. It protected corporate power, justified the use of nuclear weapons in the defense of Western Europe, justified U.S. presence there, and restored the pre-World War II social order in Western European for a twenty-five year period.

15. Richard J. Barnet, *The Giants: The United States and Russia* (New York: Simon and Schuster, 1977), pp. 110-11 (draft).

16. Joseph A. Schumpeter, *Imperialism* (New York: Meridian Books of the World Publishing Co., 1951).

17. *An Outline History of the Viet Nam Workers Party* (Hanoi: Foreign Language Publishing House, 1976), p. 159.

18. "Mao Tse Tung in an Interview with Edgar Snow," in *The Vietnam Reader*, ed. Raskin and Fall, pp. 213-16.

19. Mermelstein and Alcaly, eds., *The Fiscal Crisis of the City* (New York: Random House, 1977).

20. Roy A. Medvedev, *On Socialist Democracy* (New York: Alfred A. Knopf, 1975), pp. 53-56.

21. Ibid.

22. R.H.S. Crossman, *Socialism and the New Despotism*, "Fabian Tracts," No. 298 (London: 1956), p. 1, quoted in Friedrich A. Hayek, *The Constitution of Liberty* (Chicago: The University of Chicago Press, 1960), p. 256.

6
Imperialism Against Democracy

A peaceful democracy for American society is only possible by ending the American empire and discarding the concept of national security which buttresses that empire. National security should now be understood as the instrument used to assure the independence and freedom of the American people. Until the year 2000 and beyond, the concept of national security must include that set of understandings and mechanisms which allow Americans to undertake their own social reconstruction without outside interference. Coming down from the high of imperialism, these assertions could be viewed as novel and indeed subversive. It has long been thought by the U.S. leadership that Americans could only live with each other if they expanded their empire and engulfed their internal problems with foreign diversions. On the eve of the Civil War, Secretary of State Seward advised President Lincoln to initiate a confrontation between France and England which the United States could join with profit. This, he thought, would avert civil war in the United States and keep the nation united.

Empires act as a "safety valve for the energies of a type of personality who might become leaders of revolutions in the home territory."[1] Part of the enterprising and the privileged classes are sent abroad to seek their fortunes because their energies cannot be contained in the social system of the home territory. This begins to explain the purpose of the Peace Corps or the personal biographies of Generals Arthur and Douglas MacArthur (father and son) who, in the course of fifty years, served as the American satraps in Asia. It helps us understand the motives of those who organize global corporations when they find the limits of domestic markets.

Imperialism is often defended by the argument of superior culture. Learned journals talk of spreading better health and sanitation conditions while overlooking the painful fact that modern modes of sanitation are necessary because other imperial representatives brought their own diseases. Churches spread the religious principle of one god while business people sell the dream of consumer pleasure. They *know* full well that one god is better than many gods, or for that matter, that Coca Cola is better than sugar and water.

Until the end of the Indochina War, the practitioners and ideologues of U.S. expansion believed in "global shopping centers," protecting material resources and trade routes, and the "cult of the blood" (that indefinable quality which asserted superiority and protection over another through geographic expansion and domination of another people's consciousness). Is it not what the revolution of rising expectations came to with its creation of wants and needs? In our time, the symbols of imperial superiority include Coca Cola, nuclear reactors, and military assistance, all of which tend to justify the existence and importance of each other.

Managing an empire for profit and simultaneously fashioning an internal state structure which sets limits to domestic change is a profoundly difficult task requiring skills that are not often found in a freewheeling elite comprised of old families, specialists, super achievers, the personally ambitious, and those with great expectations. Such a freewheeling elite does not have a uniform calculator to decide benefits, pain, or utilities. Some even doubted in the early part of the twentieth century that imperialism was economically beneficial to the practicing nation. Some British writers noticed that imperialism helps particular groups within nations, but not nations as a whole with the result that imperialism tends to exacerbate internal class struggle. In our time on the international scene, imperial expansion gives rise to counter expansion and independence movements with great reliance on armaments. This usually means that a privileged warrior caste comes into being. How else can a state protect its imperial posture except, in the final analysis, than with the force of arms? It can layer a complex international economic and cultural system, but finally it must be prepared to maintain its imperial position. This requires a warrior caste with plenty of weapons and the belief that no state can stay at rest.

It is of course true that the restlessness in the United States and the belief in destiny have been greater than that of other nations. In modern times, the thirst has become virtually unquenchable. The democratic possibility fed this belief. "The picture of better and juster times has become lively in the souls of men, and a longing, a sighing for purer and freer conditions has moved hearts and set them at variance with the actuality."[2]

This condition has applied to the United States when its leaders play on the mission of the United States, its destiny, and its place as the one hope of mankind. This theme can be found in the sayings of its poets, philosophers, and presidents. It is made manifest in its immigrants who come with a dream and a scheme. Throughout U.S. history, we cling to the belief that good can be done for others while the philanthropic person or group can personally benefit. Indeed, by the 1970s a Harvard professor developed a whole scheme of justice predicated on the ability to enrich one's self if others were also enriched. Without knowing it, he was putting into philosophic concepts the ideology of growth which had reached its apogee during the post-Second World War period and was already on the decline.[3] Philosophers often catch on after the historical determinants of their thought have changed, and their ideas end up being irrelevant.

Since the New Deal, the belief has been maintained that old families with power and wealth which others attended to can be brought together with the success strivers and achievers in order to refurbish established power. It could be bolstered by merit. The merit system would fashion a new cavalier elite which would merge consciousness and function. This elite could protect its power and give the society a combination of optimism, in the personal sense of success within the social system, and skill, an ingredient necessary to manage the new economic and social governmental and corporate institutions and the empire itself.

The educations forged at the leading universities such as Harvard, Chicago, Yale, and even those in California were meant to organize society according to the new principles of merit intermixed with class.

One could see these principles operating in the mix of courses, general education (consciousness raising for the life of a gentleman or a lady), and functional majors (performance in managerial or specialized tasks). It was through this mixture of ideology and technical training that a modern imperial consciousness would be developed.

An empire requires a group consciousness which is widely shared beyong the most exalted members of the elite or at least among those who manage the apparatus of the state. Its members must calculate benefits by the same slide rule. This has been a difficult task in the United States where genuflection to democratic forms is required of even the greatest imperialists. For example, there is an uncommonly noisy public relations debate concerning equality of opportunity with proper attention paid to social mobility for the talented. But beneath the imperially created merit system meant to help the talented poor become "upward bound," all people are to believe in the natural order of rulers and ruled, dominator and dominated. This natural order is courtesy of family income and the Educational Testing Service. This imperial view cannot fit into a modern democracy for very long. A democracy is freewheeling, error-prone, passionate, requiring differences in opinion, open, and sloppy. There is an unspoken commitment to dialogue because no one group can understand or encompass the whole. It respects the limits of reason, and, therefore, it courts disrespect of authority. Leaders are pictured falling down stairs or as cripples or as nose-pickers. It would seem that the imperious Chief Justice Warren Burger is the only official able to command respect by virtue of his robe and demeanor.

In the twentieth century, an imperialist requires

more than an appearance. He needs consummate skill and command over the art of imperial inaction, a gift which Eisenhower had but which Kennedy did not possess. There is a story told about Roosevelt and Garner which reflects the instinct for imperial inaction. In the early 1930s, there was a coup-revolution in Cuba which frightened the State Department and various U.S. corporate interests. President Franklin Roosevelt sought the advice of Vice-President "Cactus Jack" Garner. Garner, who spent a great deal of time in Texas as vice-president, received a long-distance call from Roosevelt. It is said that the telephone conversation went something like this:

> Roosevelt: "Jack there has been a coup in Cuba. Should I send the marines?"
> Garner: "I'd wait."
> Roosevelt: "Suppose American property is expropriated or destroyed."
> Garner: "I'd still wait."
> Roosevelt: "But suppose an American is killed."
> Garner: "I'd wait to see which one." [4]

This type of imperial inaction may be contrasted with the performance of Ford and Kissinger during the Mayaguez incident. The United States acted unjustly and imprudently responding to the debacle at the end of the Indochina War when it appeared that the aura of U.S. invincibility was broken. U.S. leadership ordered the destruction of a number of Cambodian boats and bases ostensibly to retrieve a ship belonging to a U.S. corporation. Since the Cambodians had already agreed to return the ship, which had intelligence equipment on it, the operations were similar to the bombings of Hanoi in that they were carried out for purposes of terror and prestige. After this reprisal, the secretary of state said that the prestige and will of the United States was restored. No one was impressed. Countries that had once accepted their subservient role out of principle, profit, and fear of the military technology of the United States came to believe that they could, and indeed, had to take a more independent attitude. They do not fear reprisal in quite the same ways which they did prior to the Indochina War since such actions appear to be acts of impotence rather than of strength. Fanon had once said that the shot of salvation for the world's colonized peoples was the victory of the Vietnamese at Dien Bien Phu.[5] Twenty years later the Vietnamese freed the consciousness of the world from faith in western military technology and great power omnipotence, even as the Vietnamese, Cambodians, and Chinese restore their ancient and bloody rivalries.

The critical reason the imperialist of the twentieth century requires such superhuman skill is that imperialism flies directly against the spirit of the age. The very ideological content of twentieth century imperialism and the rhetoric used to sustain mass support (freedom, equality, fraternity, and self-determination) contradicts the imperial form. The twentieth century's cryptic nature is that its ideals seek ways to rid humanity of institutions of domination although they are often as not reproduced. That much maligned document, the Charter of the United Nations, and the resolutions passed by the General Assembly are statements of people's hope for decolonization, antiapartheid, disarmament, and reallocation of the world's wealth. Woe unto that group of imperial leaders who do not know how to relate to these aspirations, to manage them, and to be seen upholding them. The conundrum for the imperial leader is that he is required to be prudent, but the nature of imperialism is imprudent and unreasonable. Thus, in order to protect real or imagined interests, the imperialist often falls back on cruelty to show that there is an impassable gulf between the wretched and the powerful, the good doctor and the disease. How else should we explain the ordering of the Christmas terror bombing of Hanoi in 1972 by Kissinger and Nixon who knew the failure of strategic bombing as a tool in the intimidation of leaders and populations and its illegality under international law.

Cruelty and terror are only successful when one's adversaries do not have a penchant for suffering. The Indochinese were endowed with an unmasochistic form of this gift which U.S. leaders hoped to devalue using technological invincibility symbolized by sensors to smell urine, electronic battlefields to sizzle the enemy, and helicopters to pick up the dying. U.S. bureaucrats and military scientists embraced this form of technology as the elixir and shield to allow for so-called antiseptic war. The Vietnamese were diagnosed as a cancer to whom no legal or moral responsibility was attached. After all, if the enemy were not seen except as a disease, what responsibility was there to capture him or feed his family? The war itself could remain a "surgical exercise," as it was called. The modern imperialist's mode is to handle the adversary as a disease to be treated or excised. Like the violated patient, however, a liberation movement's power often stems from rage, pain, purposelessness, and rebellion inside the imperialist's armed forces, the "surgical staff" itself.

Clumsy, destructive and impatient action by the regular forces will always tend to drive civilians into the guerrilla camps. A characteristic of advanced and powerful weapons systems by land and air seems to be that, despite the allegedly 'sophisticated' electronic systems for fire control, the impression at the target is of clumsiness and purposeless destruction. For this reason, advanced weapons systems may be much more of a liability than an asset in anti-guerrilla warfare.[6]

Up until the Vietnam War, the American elite was not attuned to such arguments. Instead they believed in intelligence and social, scientific, and strategic thought. As General Maxwell Taylor put it, the empire was invincible if the American people would just try harder. Having noticed that World War II was fought in Europe and Asia, the civilians believed that the empire could afford, indeed, had to afford all manner of war—nuclear, limited, and sublimited simultaneously. It could also afford, indeed, required commercial expansion without economic controls. It needed growth of whatever kind regardless of the social and individual cost, and it needed to develop "as if" thinking which bordered on the inane, if not insane. Those in charge of national security spun farfetched policies which, when put into practice, led to pain and disaster for people. Thus, Elmo Zumwalt, former chief of naval operations, sought the coup against Allende using this mode of geopolitical reasoning.

I thought that the Soviets would be able to establish air and naval bases within a few years. If they did they could inhibit the U.S. Navy's ability to move its carriers, which are too big for the Panama Canal, from the Pacific around the Horn in a conventional war. Such bases also might serve, as Cuban missile bases might have, to provide a new axis of strategic attack by land or sea-based missiles on the United States itself.[7]

The arms race itself is an instructive lesson in the crisis of U.S. imperialism. During the cold war period, the ruling elite followed two principles. The first was that the United States needed a large armed force to maintain its empire and responsibilities abroad. This principle coincided with the need to augment the flagging internal economy of the United States which, after pent-up demand caused by the scarcity of consumer goods during the Second World War, slumped in the period of 1949-50. Fueled by the mentality of anticommunism, the arms race deepened the deformation within U.S. capitalism which encouraged an dual-sector economy. One part of that economy, for example textiles and leather, was to remain competitive while the other part, which included the largest corporations, was to be subsidized through the defense and national security sections of the federal budget.[8]

What was once dismissed as vulgar Marxism is now considered axiomatic by the most sophisticated of defense strategists with training in economics. James Schlesinger, former secretary of defense and President Carter's energy advisor, has said that arms development by the United States was an important factor in maintaining reasonably high and stable levels of employment. Ideological predilections aside, the AFL-CIO hierarchy supported Schlesinger's bid to return to the post of secretary of defense because he could guarantee high defense expenditures. Carter's choice, Harold Brown, was thought to be ignorant of the importance that the arms race played in a capitalist economy. As Sweezey and Magdoff have pointed out, the level of employment produced by the defense industries is approximately 10-12 percent of the work force. The curious and troublesome fact is that the unemployment rate of 8 percent plus the 10 percent employed in defense industries is equal to the number of unemployed the United States suffered immediately prior to the Second World War in 1939.[9]

In addition to the economic purpose of the arms race, another reason for the race was developed in the 1950s. William C. Foster, the first director of the Arms Control and Disarmament Agency, said that the arms race was intended to put pressure on the Soviet Union to develop its own defense capability. This would detract, it was thought, from its internal economic and social development. Because of the amount of energy and resources it would use for the arms race, the Soviets would not be able to develop a socialist society. It was thought that they would then give in and change—to what, however, no one quite knew. Fifteen years after this policy was first publicly formulated, it had reached absurd depths in which the United States held over 40,000 nuclear weapons, turning them out at an average of three a day. The Soviets have also built an awesome arsenal, endangering their society and the rest of the world by the sheer magnitude of their armaments. "No report can portray the enormity, the utter horror which must befall the targeted areas and adjoining territories," said the president of the Academy of Sciences,[10] and no "clean" neutron bomb will change this terrible truth.

From 1946 to 1963 Americans believed in their invincibility in the face of war and even nuclear war. An important reason for this false consciousness was their belief that the class differences within the United States were solved and that U.S. history was a liberal history in which brutality and turbulence were the exceptions rather than the rule. The liberals retained their belief in progress and believed that progress could be managed. Progress to both liberals and conservatives was analogous to an oil drum in which the oil flow could be controlled by those who had the key to the spigot. The postwar generation grew up believing in stability and thinking that the United States was not a turbulent nation. Yet any fair-minded reading of U.S. history yields exactly the reverse conclusion. One of President Johnson's commissions leaked the secret to the middle class that Americans were a violent people to others and to themselves. A staff report to the National Commission on the Causes and Preservation of Violence (the Kerner Commission) stated:

> What is to be made of this survey of violence in American history? The first and most obvious conclusion is that there is a huge amount of it. It is not merely that violence has been mixed with the negative features of our history such as criminal activity, lynch mobs, and family feuds. On the contrary violence has formed a seamless web with some of the noblest and most constructive chapters of American history: the birth of the nation (Revolutionary violence), the freeing of the slaves and the preservation of the Union (Civil War violence), the occupation of the land (Indian war), the stabilization of frontier society (vigilante violence), the elevation of the farmer and the laborer (agrarian and labor violence) and the preservation of law and order (police violence).

The study continued in a surprising vein:

> Thus American capitalist ground workers into the dust, and the result was the violent labor movement . . . . The patriot, the humanitarian, the nationalist, the pioneer, the landholder, the farmer, and the laborer (and the

capitalist) have used violence as the means to a higher end.[11]

We find that as each universal statement of progress (whether it be liberation and equality, peace and justice, participation in decision making, racial equality, even community) cannot be fulfilled through the imperial system, renewed attempts are made by malcontents to organize social existence and the politics of the society in different ways. These are often halting attempts with marginal success. While the malcontents failed in the sense of transforming or capturing power during the tumultous 1960s, the oligarchs and their administrative minions fail as mightily as they try to keep their power and continue to manage change.

There are objective and subjective reasons for this failure. The subjective reasons are not as crucial as the objective ones, but they contribute to the failure of the ruling elite to manage. The most important reason is in the nature of the American people. As some would say, there is a damnable weakness among Americans which is a search for justice and equity. Many well-to-do Americans feel guilty that they are rich and others are poor. Gunnar Myrdal has pointed out this soft streak in the American character.[12] Thus, Americans are religious in the sense that underneath their arrogance, there is a fear that they are not deserving.

More than in any other country, there are groups within the United States ready to work with third world countries in changing the relationship between rich and poor. Indeed, some of them, as shown by the Indochina War, are prepared to identify their existence with the cause of the wretched. This is, of

course, a surprise to many conservative mandarins
who do not believe in world progress and do not comprehend this spirit of justice within Americans. One
such mandarin, Robert Tucker of Johns Hopkins
University, wondered why so many intellectuals
were traitors to their class, wanted to share with
others, and sought means of shifting the international social structure which would cause them to suffer.
But another American mandarin takes the side of
terrorist groups around the world. Robert Clark, the
Adolph Ochs Professor of Political Science, cannot
understand why gangs of terrorists who have legitimate political demands should be shunned. He wants
their demands for liberation to be taken seriously.
This urge for justice which finds its way into the
nation's attitudes is hard to extirpate because it ful-
fills America's sense of mission and commitment that
some people have for the wretched. It is especially
difficult to curb because of the constitutional right of
free speech and association. As Joseph Schumpeter
once remarked, free speech would end up undoing
capitalism and the capitalist system.[13] It has been the
informer's role to protect against free speech and
political deviance.

There is much evidence to show that police informers involved themselves in assassination plots, encouraged bombings of facilities, and often attempted
to entrap the dissidents and earlier movements into
foolish actions which would result in their apprehen-
sion and isolation from their supporters or the
citizenry at large. Police informers acted as a little-
understood force. They operated sometimes for and
sometimes against their employers and the state apparatus. Perhaps there was an answer to this puzzle
in psychology. The informer, confused and without

status in the world as a lumpen character, is open to personal blackmail. He seeks to transcend his situation by turning it into one of adventure, notoriety, and double-dealing. As it turned out, the informers were especially active and successful in distorting the personal relationships of people in the various movements of the 1960s and in creating doubt and spreading paranoia. The informer is critical to the operations of the twentieth century state, in the East and West alike. He represents the difference between the person who is a citizen and acts with a true face and an agent-employee who has surrendered his true face. All states vacillate on whether they want employee-informers or citizens. The United States is no exception. But we should not conclude that informing was circumscribed to SDS. It was critical to politics at the highest levels of the government. Throughout the cold war period, it was taken for granted that one agency eavesdropped on another and that the members of Congress and their aides were bugged.

The cousin to such activity is bribery. This instrument of paying for evidence, or paying informers and agents of other countries including government officials has long been a practice of states. The American middle class, however, did not believe that U.S. officials could be bribed by agents of other states. Although it was taken for granted that the CIA or other intelligence agencies could and should buy the parliaments of other countries, it was not contemplated by the American people that other intelligence agencies would be able to successfully buy or rent U.S. politicians in Congress. Americans are often blinded by patriotic pronouncements of politicians, but their blindfolds have been cut away as they learned that members of Congress received payments on a regular basis from the South Korean CIA or that the Iranians now employ former CIA director Richard Helms. Whether the U.S. national security apparatus picked out the congressional recipients of foreign largesse is also unknown. What we all learned was that the sort of killings and assassinations which were initiated or acquiesced abroad were now performed on the streets of Washington either as an affront or warning to the American government.

In the twentieth century, American society has not known how to shake either imperial pretension or the growth of modern capitalism. Both of these forces have impoverished the civil society to the point where cities and states such as New York and Pennsylvania are unable to meet their obligations to employees. The city of Detroit went to the federal government to find ways of meeting their unemployment problems although no one bothers the great automobile makers with such questions. It is well to mention the impoverishment of our culture resulting from the type of economic system we fashioned. The automobile industry reflects our problems and contradicitons. Henry Ford II, in a book entitled *Freedom of the American Road*, said that "we Americans always have liked plenty of elbow room—freedom to come and go as we please in this big country of ours."[14] This ideology required that American cities become secondary to the mammoth automobile industry just as the national security system became more important than the people.

As American cities became the launching pads for the highway system, a public transportation authorities system was developed outside the purview of city control. Robert Moses said:

> The great need is for mixed traffic expressways right
> through town. These are prodigious undertakings, the
> full extent and nature of which the average city dweller
> does not yet grasp. Probably most people with their
> minds elsewhere will not realize what is in store until
> they are disturbed and discommoded by demolition,
> moving of tenants, and the inevitable noise, dust, exca-
> vation and detours of heavy construction . . . . Once the
> plan is set in motion 'the rest' is battling obstructionists,
> moving people and dirt paving, planting, veneering and
> painting the lily.[15]

General Motors worked out a successful scheme to
destroy more than a hundred electric surface rail
transit systems in forty-five cities including Baltimore, Los Angeles, New York, Philadelphia, and St.
Louis between 1932 and 1956. The predatory nature
of the automobile industry has meant a continued
destruction of the cities and the countryside. This is a
question which the major political parties and
philosophers do not care to address. The tragic nature
of the automobile industry is reflected in workers
arguing for minimum pollution control standards because they fear loss of income and jobs. This is an
indirect form of economic blackmail. It is reflected in
the increased dependence on oil and energy sources
from outside the United States.

The shift in concerns in the United States regard-
ing its imperial position is caused by a new consciousness in the international economic system
which demands more for the poor and less for the rich
nations. Since 1970 a greater organized awareness
and "objective understandings of economic realities,"
have been formulated in U.N. resolutions. The most
important of these proclaimed an International Economic Order built on principles of equity, sovereign

equality, common interest, peace, justice and narrow-
ing the gap between rich and poor nations. Once
alliances shift in world politics, words which were
usually thought of as rhetorical or precatory take on a
much more lively meaning.

The changes in the world balance are reflected in
U.N. studies which were conducted to show how the
International Economic Order could be accomplished. It was taken for granted in this study that
developing countries would expand and double their
share of GNP and that the developed centrally-
planned economies (the socialist economies) would
develop at "a rate somewhat higher than the world
average and their share in the world total would also
increase. Most of the developed market economies
would expand at rates *below* world averages, and
their total share would decrease to about half as compared with the present two-thirds."[16] This means
that the economic situation within the United States
will become increasingly tight unless redistribution
plans and value changes are initiated within the
United States over the next generation. Without such
changes, resource wars for oil or minerals could occur. Imperial leaders including Johnson, Nixon, and
Kissinger believed that sacrifice must be made
through national security institutions which are
meant to protect wasteful and imperial ways. The
CIA and other defense institutions were seen as institutions to coopt and control the leadership of other
nations which would accept U.S. profligacy and primacy while playing down the needs of their own people. Leaders of nations are bribed by great corporations to obtain special treatment and control over the
economy and consciousness of their countries.
Through the military and economic assistance pro-

grams, the corporations and the military have attempted to make the business classes of other nations part of the international pyramid of rulers with the Americans retaining top position. But the scheme is not thought to be a very successful one, and the reasons are obvious. Internally in the United States, not enough groups gain from imperialism in a direct sense. Externally, other nations have come to understand that without the possibility of major scientific breakthroughs on the use of metal substitutes, third world nations could limit the mineral appetite of the United States.

While this is not the place to discuss the question of how the shift in the perception of world power has occurred, the old relationship between the users and producers of resources is being broken. In the past, producers were kept to one crop for the benefit of the industrialized country so that the producers would become reliant for their existence on that one crop. But as all relationships show, history is ironic. In hierarchic relationships, the master becomes dependent on the slave and both are shocked. It was never contemplated that the industrialized countries would become equally dependent on the poor nations. This happened once industrialized nations and their leadership classes gave up Puritanism and any interest in controlling and limiting their technological and resource needs.

By suggesting that elites in the United States have a boundless appetite, I am constrained to say that there is little which Americans hold to be "sacred ground." In previous empires leaders held to a fixed point. In the United States, however, until Carter was elected, U.S. leaders found that their collective compass was broken. The educational system in the

United States assumes that there is no fixed point
beyond the natural growth of narrow economic,
power, and specialized interests. Transfixed by technology and gadgetry which they encouraged and controlled, U.S. leaders have failed to realize how technology itself dictates foolish judgments. It became
harder and harder to comprehend the meaning of
interests, whether short-term or long-term, since the
modes of rational calculations are very difficult when
change is worshipped as a good in itself. There is no
measuring device.[17]

We should not think that this generation is the
only one that has concerned itself with value shifts
and programmatic alternatives. At the turn of the
century in the United States, there were strong radical groupings including socialists, anarchists, and
populists who believed that the government had to
step forward to regulate or to take over major U.S.
industries. Socialist and anarchist voices were dealt
with in Bismarckian fashion: the group as well as the
doctrine could be tamed. The idea of regulating industry was adopted by Theodore Roosevelt and Wilson, and it became part of a watered-down form of
liberalism. That part which could not be tamed or
controlled was declared outside of political dialogue
and dealt with accordingly. For example, after the
First World War, Wilson's attorney general ordered
the pickup and expulsion from the United States of
some 10,000 radical, socialist, and anarchist aliens.
Socialist and anarchist ideas were excluded from the
course of political debate and consigned to discussions among those who were considered to be de-
viants, irresponsible, and irrelevant. Radicals were
seen as ideological criminals and therefore a problem
for the police and later the FBI. When liberal lawyers
defended them in court, they invariably did so on

procedural grounds. They refrained from addressing the arguments of the radicals who were considered misguided folk. It was in this way that the United States was inoculated against radical ideas for a period of over fifty years.

While radical politics were declared criminal, citizen politics in the sense of deliberation and execution of choice were deemed unworkable. It was assumed that the serious work of society would go on behind closed doors by bureaucrats, administrators, and representatives of the largest interest groups. Bureaucracy would be continuous, and it would undertake to make the welter of ad hoc decisions of the president and the Congress into a so-called framework of rationality which would be the central way in which decisions were made. In this process, the concerns of citizens would be taken care of through administrative decisions. They would be serviced; in clever administrations, they would even be given access but not the deliberating and implementing power as citizens.

As I have suggested elsewhere, the political situation in the United States yields contradictions and ironies. Those in bureaucracy insist that their power is derived and illusory. The average citizen believes that bureaucratic power is crucial and decisive. Whatever people's subjective feelings may be, it is clear that the administrative and indeed the national security state has grown to the point that it is central in the everyday life of Americans. As the economist James O'Connor has pointed out, the dependence of the state as an instrument runs very deep in all classes:

At present, the United States federal government employs about 2.5 million civilian workers in eighty de-

partments and agencies and nearly 4 million members
of the armed forces, and total state and local government employment is 8.5 million. In the federal government, employment is greatest in military and international relations agencies and the postal service, which
employ 1 million and 600,000 workers, respectively. At
the state and local levels, employment is concentrated
in the fields of education (4 million workers), health and
hospitals (1 million), highways (520,000) and police protection (450,000). In addition to the 11 million workers
employed directly by the state, there are countless wage
and salary earners—perhaps as many as 25 to 30
million—who are employed by private capital dependent in whole or in part on state contracts and facilities.
This does not include those dependent on the budget as
clients and recipients of state services in education,
welfare, recreation, etc.[18]

The power of bureaucracy and the state was further
increased when Congress turned over to the president and the state apparatus enormous grants of authority. There are some 470 provisions of federal law
that delegate to the president extraordinary powers.
This power, coupled with the so-called inherent powers of the president, give him carte blanche to act as
he sees fit:

> Under the power delegated by these statutes, the Presi-
> dent may: seize property; organize and control the
> means of production; seize commodities; assign military
> forces abroad; institute martial law; seize and control
> all transportation and communication; regulate the op-
> eration of private enterprise; restrict travel; and, in a
> plethora of particular ways, control the lives of all
> American citizens.[19]

Such powers can in theory give a president the right

to transform the state apparatus into virtually anything he wants.

The temporary success of Congress in cutting back presidential power as evidenced in various pieces of emergency legislation will no doubt be short-lived in President Carter's governmental reorganization plans. No governmental reorganization proposal since the Brownlow Commission of 1939 has successfully increased the accountability of the executive to Congress. There is now, however, a double irony which will grip U.S. politics for the rest of the twentieth century. A persuasive case can be made that the power of the president (the person) has grown weaker as the power of the executive (the presidency) has increased. There have been two forced resignations from the presidency, and one president was assassinated in fifteen years. While Congress used the Vietnam War and Nixon's experience to restore some of its institutional power as a coordinate branch of government, it has not done so with progressive, substantive programs. Quite to the contrary, the Congress seeks to find the centrist-rightist mean and criticizes the administration. It is uninterested in problems of redistribution, limitation of armaments, or other issues which would tend to give a progressive cast to the Democratic Party. But for the Right, most members of Congress are organized in their daily activities *against* the party program. Their daily lives are similar to those of small business entrepreneurs competing against one another, committed to the sport of politics, where they are committed, and fearful of a political process which might result in ending imperialism, or bringing democratic participation and economic justice.

NOTES

1. Quincy Wright, *A Study of War* (Chicago: The University of Chicago Press, 1942), pp. 1189-92 and 828-29.

2. T.M. Knox, trans. *Hegel's Political Writings*, (New York: Oxford Press, 1964), p. 224.

3. John Rawls, *A Theory of Justice* (Cambridge: The Belknap Press of Harvard University Press, 1971).

4. Ernest K. Lindley, *The New Dealers* (New York: Simon and Schuster, 1934), pp. 280-81.

5. Frantz Fanon, *The Wretched of the Earth* (New York: Grove Press, Inc., 1968).

6. Vladimir Dedijer, "The Poor Man's Power," in *Unless Peace Comes*, ed. Nigel Calder (New York: Viking Press, 1968), p. 37.

7. Elmo Zumwalt, *On Watch* (New York: Quadrangle Books, 1976), p. 322.

8. The reader is referred to the study of the Defense Department of the largest defense corporations, noted in chapter three above. I would add that with the failure of the U.S. economy to achieve full employment, state subsidy for high employment is critical. The only question is what type of subsidy will occur. Would it be the kind which would change the balance of power within American society as was outlined in President Roosevelt's 1944 state of the union address which called for eight basic economic rights, or would it be obtained in other ways?

9. Sweezy and Magdoff, *The Dynamics of American Capitalism*, pp. 51-53.

10. *Long-Term Worldwide Effects of Multiple Nuclear Weapons*, National Academy of Sciences Report, October 1976.

11. *National Commission on the Causes and Prevention of Violence* (Washington: Government Printing Office, 1968), p. 55.

12. Gunnar Myrdal, *Challenge to Affluence* (New York: Pantheon Books, 1963).

13. Joseph A. Schumpeter, *Capitalism, Socialism and Democracy*, 3d ed., (New York: Harper and Row, 1950).

14. Henry Ford, *Freedom of the American Road*; quoted in Kenneth Schneider, *Autokind vs. Mankind* (New York: Schocken Books, 1971), p. 85.

15. Robert Moses in Schneider, *Autokind vs. Mankind*, p. 94-95.

16. Wassily Leontief et al., *The Future of the World Economy*, United Nations Report, January 1977.

17. John Rawls; Robert Nozick, *Anarchy, State and Utopia* (New York: Basic Books, Inc., Publishers, 1974), pp. 167-74. Attempts have been made by Rawls and Nozick to build on the calculative mode of interest believing that interest on money and personal interest added up to the immanent mode of measuring interest.

18. James O'Connor, *The Corporations and the State: Essays in the Theory of Capitalism and Imperialism* (New York: Harper and Row, Publishers, 1974), pp. 105-6.

19. United States Senate, Committee on the Termination of the National Emergency Senators Charles Mathias and Frank Church, Forward in *Emergency Power Statutes: Provisions of Federal Law Now in Effect Delegating to the Executive Extraordinary Authority in Time of National Emergency*, 19 November 1973 (Washington: Government Printing Office, 1973), p. iii.

7
A Different Focus

There is only the most inchoate view of an alternative to the national security state and imperialism because the required steps are such profound ones. These steps must be toward political and economic democracy, forms of public enterprise, and forms of what used to be called "the common." I would prefer that we not worry about the political name, but look at the processes to be initiated and strengthened in this reconstruction. If it needs a name, I think modern reconstruction is the most fitting. What is critical, however, is that questions concerning property be answered in new ways.

The latter twentieth and twenty-first century meaning of the common has a different connotation than it did in the eighteenth century. The common once meant those lands to be shared in order that private ownership could be protected or enhanced. But in our time, we are required to ask what is to be held in common in the cities before inequalities are countenanced. Since this means directly confronting the class structure, there is the political problem that great discomfort will be generated among the rich, the trustees of the newly rich, or that section of the middle class which assigns its success to personal hard work or natural merit and endowments. Serious discussions are required within these sectors so that attempts at economic distribution will not be sabotaged. Distribution schemes often fail because they are not preceded by discussions on value and purpose. Even the organized segments of the working class fear change because they feel they will be the group that will end up paying for economic distribution. Their experience is that the rich are far better organized to withstand economic attack on their privileges.

Some make the argument that the arms race and the threat of war sustain the present internal and external power configuration. It is terrifying that the United States will most likely spend a trillion dollars on defense during 1977-82. In addition, there is the horror that if a nuclear war is fought, it would destroy the American society itself and the likelihood that those who would order the use of nuclear weapons would be known as civilization's arch war criminals. The problem is Congressmen Brademas, Bolling, and Stevenson or Secretary of State Vance or closet socialist trade union leaders would have to abandon the fundamental assumptions of the last generation. They would have to embrace an alternative course, and they would have to give up their romance with capitalism and empire. They would have to disavow the assumptions of the last generation and the misplaced belief that the U.S. corporation and military are disguised instruments of revolutionary idealism (a position dearly held in the Carter administration). But which way the liberals will turn is unclear. Their ideological course will depend, in my view, on

whether or not a progressive populist movement de-
velops in this country separate from those who saw
themselves as liberal.

Such a movement should seek easily understood
objectives: that everybody is entitled to work, that
individual accumulation is secondary to the development of the common, that citizenship means
egalitarianism in result, and privilege is recognized
to the extent it enhances the common good, and that
citizenship must now extend as well to the work
place. In the context of such objectives to be fully
explored for their consequences, the populist movement in the United States should take up the basic
question of militarism. This means unraveling the
arms system. A series of slogans which could be propounded directly by people in the universities and
debated in the factories and other places of work and
on the streets would then cause liberals to make their
intentions clear. This strategy has been successful in
the civil rights, the anti-Indochina War, and women's
rights movements.

If there is no group to organize the consciousness or
dissatisfaction and dissonance in a positive direction,
there will indeed be a steady urban decline, inability
to deal with the problems of the economy and the
bureaucratic fascist elements of the national security
state will be strengthened. It will take the obvious
authoritarian form—the centralizing of the police
system internally and an attempt to develop internal
passport systems in the country which is already
encouraged by the passport division. They now suggest that everbody should carry a national identity
card. Of course, public school children and factory
workers already need passports to leave their schools
and factories. Can this direction be interrupted? To a

very great extent, it depends on whether people can transcend the consciousness of dissatisfaction to forge an intelligent, hopeful program that fits the needs of the time.

This type of program will place a strain on liberalism. Since the New Deal, virtually all liberal political ideas assumed a strong leadership from a president who was symbolic of positive historical forces. He shaped those forces with an economic and cultural program that would make better music for certain forms of monopoly and oligopoly capitalism than capitalism is otherwise able to do. Nevertheless, there are other policies of liberalism which reject the partnership theory of government with private capital and the military. These perspectives were closer to those found in pacifist social democracy and socialism.

Eugene Debs, Upton Sinclair, Robert La Follette, Sr., and John Dewey all believed that workers would have to exercise control of the work place. They showed a deep suspicion of wealth privately held and a deep suspicion of leaders who took their people to war. This type of liberalism, which was humanistic and pragmatic in the sense that it aimed at good ends beyond the class system was washed out in the 1940s as a result of fear of the Soviet Union, state power, and the success of the United States in the Second World War. Liberalism lost its independent moorings once it vectored toward the state and the corporation with technocratic expertise and avoided populism or socialist ideas. Pragmatist thought which liberals championed was reduced to questions of strategy for changes which were described as incremental. Their effects, however, were far reaching but less affirmative than any suggested systemic changes. One may note how changing the transportation system or providing health care for everyone has had the most profound indirect effects. Because we think in terms of piecemeal programs, we wrongly think that they have only limited effect.

As a political matter, we should criticize and organize against false incrementalism and the politics that justify the present formula to protect state and corporate power. They are little more than role-hugging, and they will solve nothing. In practical terms, our reforms will merely reflect the continuing and deepening horror of the arms race and the massive economic insecurity of the American people. Such personal and ideological role hugging encourages isolation from the social rhythm of the world and results in the deepened stratification and segmentation of American society. Since these arguments can be easily demonstrated, the development of prudential alternatives will be heard if such debates are extended throughout the society into classrooms, labor halls, and newspapers. And that, it seems to me, is one course that should be pursued by those intent on developing a progressive program. In part, the media served this educational function during the Indochina War. In television reporting of that war from 1967 until its tragic end in which refugee children were killed in a U.S. plane as it took off, there was an invariable contradiction between what was said by the government spokesman and what was shown in the films of the war. The viewers internalized those pictures even more than they internalized the vacuous talk of the newscasters.

People in modern society are serialized—that is, they are divided from each other with very little public space in which people can do things together.

In the ordinary course of today's life, we may conclude too quickly that it is almost impossible to find constituencies for the purpose of political transformation toward a new common. One reason, of course, is that there are large numbers of people who are the incarcerated and caretakers. They are in jails, insane asylums, schools, nursing homes, and armies. In other words, they are in places where the outward appearance is that they are beyond the pale and have no ideas or views other than that of their institutional place. On the contrary, they have a great deal of time to sit, think, and talk with one another. The problems about which the people sit, think, and talk usually fall into two categories. Much or all of the inmates' talk is quite paranoid, segmented, and broken and the other talk reflects their experience and the need for profound change. This concern goes up and down the pyramid of the bureaucratic system: from the hospital worker to the chief of staff of the hospital to the patient, from the school child and teacher to the school superintendent, from the soldier to the sergeant to the general, and from the petty bureaucrat to the policy maker.

In a period before great social transformation, there is no public dialogue about what to do. There is instead a private understanding among institutions that things and processes are not working and that things have to be different. In the second stage, people come forward with plans, programs, and alternatives and publicly state their disrespect and need for something else. My view is that we are now in the second stage. Young city and state representatives are searching for alternatives. One such important program is that of the Conference on State and Local Alternatives, brilliantly organized by Lee Webb and

others. There are people who have been working on
alternatives as in the case of the Exploratory Project
on Economic Alternatives of Gar Alperovitz and Jeff
Faux or those who worked with me on *The Federal
Budget and Social Reconstruction*; there are people
who represent this new wave and whose analysis and
moral sensibility have been exemplary in this last
generation. It was the antiwar movement which
promulgated a moral and political alternative to the
standards of leadership and served as the demise of
the Nixon-Agnew administration. This allows us to
see potentiality and hope. Americans are often seen
as very selfish; they are seen as tied to the fruits of
imperialism which they are prepared to struggle for
against everybody, including the rest of the world
and their own wretched. I do not agree. There is a
great deal of wisdom in people. The only problem is in
finding means of communication. Scholars, activists,
and intellectuals can form networks outside of the
schools through dialogue in order that two-way communication can begin to develop among different
groups. As we talk, I am struck by the fact that we feel
ourselves to be at a critical turn in the road. The two
major political parties are, presently, status quo parties. They are uninterested in systemic transformation, and their workers are mystified by the imperial
structure and hopeful that a check on inflation will
keep the volatile upper middle class constituency
loyal to the two party system.

One of the great struggles of this next period will
concern the question of social fascism. The national
security policies will continue to be aggressive internationally. In this process, imperial activists such as
Daniel Moynihan are seeking ways to rip away the
mask of liberalism and enunciate a Spartan policy at

home and an aggressive worldwide stance to assure
the primacy of the United States over world raw
materials. The position that is taken by those who
favor an imperial offense, from Nitze to Schlesinger
and Jackson, is that it is the national security apparatus which benefits the American people in the
most basic sense, from the Rockefellers to the Mississippi tenant farmers.

Senator Jackson has argued that prosperity in the
United States is entirely dependent on its empire and
that the national security state is the organizational
muscle that makes this possible. But the economic
and social reality contradicts this opinion—an opinion very popular in a large segment of the Democratic
Party. There is a decline in the actual material base
of the society and an increase in meaningless work,
inflation, and structural underemployment. There is
a top-heavy bureaucracy which grows larger as its
direction and purpose is limited to the reproduction of
itself. The bureaucratic task in national security becomes the justification for the uses of force in an
updated version of military brinksmanship. This
means that from time to time the United States will
use its military force, be it nuclear weapons or B-52s
on objects of our choice. It means for those trained in
the abstractions of geopolitics an active military
strategy of showing the flag through aid and military
forces throughout the world.

All of these activities assume an inert populace.
They assume the perpetuation of a power structure
which will be able to act without opposition. They
assume that the leading Wall Street bankers, the
corporate executives, leading lawyers, and military
will continue to operate in agreement with each other
according to some ideology that is understood, can be

easily taught, and can be swallowed by the media, intellectual classes, and labor leaders. This ideology does not now exist, nor can it. Brzezinski's revolutionary ideology for the status quo is a poor substitute for social transformation. The cultural hegemony of the national security state is severely tarnished, although, as I have suggested, by expanding its horizons to include problems that mask the questions of domination inherent in them, it will be able to generate some support among the upper middle class and the universities. Support in this class, however, should not be construed as general support. The payoffs get smaller and smaller and the costs of getting those payoffs continue to increase. A highly trained university graduate who thought that there was a place for him in the national security structure now finds otherwise, just as the relationship between interests and resources used for those interests is one which may be in Schlesinger's or Brown's head but in few others. There doesn't seem to be a direct relationship, for example, between a B-1 bomber, a Poseidon, and the average person's or city's interests except as economic livelihood in the cities where those weapons are made.

Even though there is no strong disarmament movement now, the fact of the matter is that the arms budget is recognized as a make-work system in the society. There is an astonishing quality to the dynamics of armaments. The production of major weapons systems continues on a massive scale despite inflation and a declining level of economic activity in most industrialized countries. There is little question, as the yearbook of the Stockholm International Peace Research Institute (SIPRI) points out, that the U.S. defense budget is "deliberately expanded" to boost the economy.[1] As James Tobin, a former member of the council of economic advisors, has pointed out:

> The sheer size of defense expenditures even when they are matched dollar for dollar by taxes, is an expansionary economic influence. The reason is that taxes are paid at the expense of saving as well as of spending. To put the point another way, if government expenditures were lowered by, say, $25 billion (from the defense budget) it would be necessary to cut tax receipts by more than $25 billion—perhaps $30 billion—in order to induce taxpayers to replace the $25 billion of government spending with $25 billion of their own spending. This means that if government expenditures were substantially lower, we would probably need *more* frequent and *larger* budget deficits to maintain prosperity and high employment.[2]

In a somewhat different context, Tobin points out that "keeping up with the Russians in missiles is just a substitute for keeping up with the Joneses in advertised gadgets."[3]

When societies undertake pathological directions, they often rationalize them with arguments that no other direction is possible. After the bubonic plague, Pericles told those Athenians who wanted to pull out of the Peloponnesian War that it was too late for them to play the part of peacelovers and honest men because they had created an empire and were hated everywhere. They were despised not only for their cultural flowering and possessions but for what they had done to others. It is Pericles' ideology that will be fearlessly used by jingoistic and "up front" imperialists to justify the national security state. Thus, we have Senator Moynihan speaking like a modern day Spengler sounding the alarm to protect our version of western civilization from the Tartar hordes. I am not convinced that Americans see themselves as imperialists or identify their interests with those of various U.S.-owned oil corporations. Although the seven sisters charged Americans less for oil than the prices they set in other nations, it will not be long before most consumers learn that it is not OPEC which controls the actual price and marketing system for oil but the great oil corporations.

Even various ruling elites see that the benefits they receive from imperialism are far fewer than the costs. As we have seen, when this fact was noticed by various business leaders, the pegs of support were pulled from the Indochina War. There could be a split within the business class between those who operate abroad and smaller operators who, for reasons of capital investment, must remain based in the United States. The attempt of the Carter administration to paper over these differences by listening sympathetically to the pluralistic views of competing groups will merely increase long-term contradictions as citizens learn they do not have producer power. It can be argued that there is no antagonistic contradiction between Warnke and Nitze or between Young and Stennis. However, I doubt that there is any transcendent set of principles, no matter how spiritually stated, which will allow such viewpoints to forge a coherent ruling ideology which the leaders can believe or the citizens accept.

Suppose there developed an imperial ruling class in the United States of the calibre of Pericles, and it said, "We know where we are, this is what we have to do, these are our interests, these are our commitments, and we are prepared to do what is necessary for our purposes. What matters is not freedom, but security and dominance." The fact still remains that the imperialism of Eisenhower, the most prudent imperialist, was hardly in Pericles' class, and we must remember that Pericles was central to the undoing of Athens. The present ruling class is even less capable of deciding what its limits and commitments are because of splits and differences in interest among them. Panel reports of foundations and polling of elites do not generate binding ideology. In addition, case studies of bureaucratic politics merely organize the common law of error. Furthermore, there is genuine confusion about specific problems. Do managers and leaders favor the Hanoi Communists over the Maoists? Saudi Arabia over Egypt? Upwardly mobile, pragmatic blacks over cold war anticommunist union leaders?

With such questions to answer, it is no wonder that those concerned with stability seek technical expertise for their answers. Ironically, the stability view is partly a Marxist legacy. Marxists believed, as did Lenin, that politics was the reflection of the struggle between classes. Parliaments were there for the struggle of different classes. They believed that once a revolution occurred, politics would end. In its place, scientific administration would devise scientific and rational means for making judgments and distributing goods and services. The rational administrator would even develop grand purposes for the society.

Scientific administration would include technocrats as well as party people who would control the direction or objectives of the people. But these assumptions are shared by the status quo as well. The national security state starts from the same set of assumptions. The managers assumed that politics was corrupt, divisive, and petty. Administration was the only correct way to develop priorities, purposes, and objectives integrated by a scientific methodology. Harold Brown, the architect of the marginal utility of bombing schemes in the Indochina War and the secretary of defense in the Carter administration, is trusted throughout the bureaucracy for his technical skills and their application to genocide, weaponry, and war fighting. This form of technocratic expertise and the national security state are inseparable.

Out of the nature of the weaponry grows the need to calculate and amass huge resources for particular ends. In one sense, each missile, submarine, and armed division is like a pharoanic pyramid whose mysteries may well be hard to repeat in a less necrophilic time because such ideas of organization will seem utterly mad. In our time, the national security state became the deformed mirror image of Marxist-Weberian principles of politics and administration. Our leading thinkers believed that politics could be replaced by administration. In the United States, men such as Harold Lasswell have thought that policy sciences could replace politics, and the administrator would carry into the dusty halls of government buildings the quantitative tools of the social sciences which would need no assumptions other than those that were hidden and uncontested. Thus, society and its institutions were calculated in a frozen form just as wars were calculated without the willingness to break the ice so that the horror under the surface could be exposed.

This dessicated form of politics will doom man. Politics is not only symbolized by a struggle between classes or a Roman aristocrat's struggle to fulfill his ambition; it is the instrument that we ordinarily think of as hope. It is the means to overcome the box of tragedies including our own and those of others. It is the gift of action which urges us to assert our existence. Politics and hope are inseparable because they link possibility to necessity and action in our lives.

Politics in this sense means recognizing the transient value of comfort and class privilege. Both of these are poker chips to be risked and lost for purposes that grow out of the necessity of others and shared potentiality. When this political meaning is not present in the minds of those who believe in reconstruction, immobilism and a paralyzing fear set in when dealing with the powerful and vicious.

The mature radicals of the 1940s and early 1950s were conscious of economic affluence and were pleased by it. Many of them had come through the terrifying 1930s—a time of great personal economic insecurity. To return to the depression standards after the Second World War must have been a frightening thing for them. They believed that liberals and the Left would support them and not allow them to be cast out of the system. Instead, they were isolated by the liberals and to a very great extent, destroyed by them.

A generation ago, too many of the old Left allied themselves with the Soviet Union in an utterly uncritical way. It took an unconscionably long time to discover that the Soviet Union was a frozen bourgeois state encased in the rhetoric of revolution and committed to unrequited brutality. Stalin represented a profound regressive force, and neither the American Communist Party nor part of the Left could come to grips with that fact.

A generation later, there are different leftist groups around the world which one can study and comprehend their mistakes or reject totally. We are in a position to say that we can do things differently because we have a high material base and realize the importance of middle class freedom which is a *sine qua non* for future social transformation. Such freedom allows for a progressive American alternative to emerge from our culture and our traditions. One might say that this is even mandated.

There is another fear which is no longer present. A generation ago, so many of the people who formed the Left were either immigrants or children of immigrants. It was easy for them to internalize their own disloyalty because they did not know that as citizens they had the right and responsibility to define the meaning of loyalty and disloyalty. In other words, they accepted a colonized status, and they accepted the principle and consciousness of the colonizer. They acted like prisoners and the guilty. Today, however, the situation is very different. Those who struggled hardest against the Indochina War or against imperialism or against economic deprivation believe that they are the ones who are loyal to the most important practical ideals of this country and to the development of democracy and liberation. A liberated consciousness not only changes people's sense of who they are individually, but it also changes a collective possibility. This potentiality of power has not yet translated itself into the work structure of the assembly line or corporate office.

Yet, as I have said, the United States is a Hegelian society in the sense that people are invariably trying to concretize human ideals. Although the process and conclusion are sometimes grotesque, perverted, and often humorous, the impulse is present. While the Left was excluded from political debate in the 1950s

and early 1960s, those people who would have otherwise found themselves in a leftist political party involved themselves in discrete causes for human ideals. Each by itself seemed unexceptionable and well
within the consensus. However, as each idealistic
impulse was attempted in practice, it challenged the
state apparatus and the blanket of consensus of the
society. Furthermore, they suggested a profound
process of radical reconstruction when added together.

The demise of the New Deal and the failure to
organize a national party of the Left in 1948 meant
that those people who would have ordinarily favored
a coherent program on matters from health to defense
limited their interest in politics to a single issue.
There was a pragmatic reason for this. Anyone who
favored more than one cause from a leftist perspec-
tive (such as civil rights and disarmament) was
thought of as a dangerous radical beyond the bounds
of debate in polite society. One could be for civil rights
and against disarmament as was Senator Paul Douglas of Illinois or for disarmament and against civil
rights as was Senator J. William Fulbright of Arkan-
sas but not for both at the same time without being
accused of subversion.

The two-party system was meant to weld issues
and people giving them either status or the appearance of participation so that no group would coalesce
around a different world view and realize itself as a
national political party. The social movements which
shook the American consciousness in the 1950s and
1960s would have ben the basis of a new political
party in other nations in western or northern Europe.
But due to the power of the individual states through
election laws and police surveillance to harass those

who sought changes coupled with the national liberal consensus that social movements should remain separate one from the other for greater effectiveness, it has been virtually impossible until now to develop a coherent and progressive program from the movements of the last several decades. We see, however, that each movement needs the work and understanding of other movements just because of the interrelated nature of problems. Equal rights means little without full employment; full employment means little if it is based on a war economy; and more schools mean nothing if what is learned in them positively harms the child. It would be well to review the movements which did erupt leaving us with the question of whether they can be brought into a coherent program which would not be destroyed or deflected by the new stage of the national security state.

The major movements of the late 1950s and 1960s which shook American consciousness included civil rights, student alienation, antiwar protest, personal liberation and the counterculture, women's rights, consumer doubts, and environmental despoliation. Each movement was different although all had in common the fact that the participants felt that there was a subjective dissonance between the way in which they experienced reality and the way in which it was described by the consensus.

The civil rights movement brought Ghandian techniques of struggle to the United States to break down apartheid. These techniques together with the support of desegregation by the legitimate federal institutions, the Supreme Court and the presidency, gave legitimacy to the power of the black movements. New federal laws were found or fashioned to justify civil disobedience. This struggle was understood by blacks and the managers of the national security state as part of a worldwide decolonization. This is why in the early 1950s the State Department attempted to show at least in a propagandistic way that the United States was antiracist through confronting apartheid laws. The United States would not win its propaganda war with communism if legal segregation persisted in the United States. Martin Luther King, Jr. adverted to the international decolonization struggle by saying that it must now continue in the United States. King had said in 1962 that the black "sense of inadequacy is heightened when they look at Africa and Asia and see with envy the bursting of age-old bonds in societies still partially at tribal level, but ablaze with modern vitality and creativity. An Alliance for Progress for the turbulent South is equally necessary."[3] Of course, neither happened. Ironically, Andrew Young, King's deputy in those years, now uses the experience of the United States to show Africans how they should continue their liberation struggles. The civil rights movement in the United States, in its nonviolent stage and in the riots of the cities, made clear that a new definition of equality and citizenship had to be fashioned within the United States if it intended to be a democracy in reality. This latter question, the meaning in political and economic terms of U.S. citizenship, remains unanswered and is central to the next stage in U.S. history. The entire issue of citizenship has been opened up by Chicanos and American Indians as they seek to clarify their control of land and culture in the United States. The Poor People's Campaign of 1968, led by King, reflected a double test. It tested whether revolutionary nonviolence was possible as a major instrument for economic redistribution, and it raised the question of whether the Bill of Rights included economic rights. "The action was to be carefully phased into strategies of mounting militancy that would have, quite simply, prevented the nation's business from being conducted in Washington, if that what was required to get response to the demands of the poor."[4] But the successful merging which Martin King brought about in 1965 between the antiwar movement and the civil rights movement was not successful when it came to economic rights for the poor and parts of the working class. He was assassinated in Memphis the night before he was to lead a march of sanitation workers.

While most blacks felt themselves to be colonized (that is, landless and without property or status and living out lives that the system laid onto them), young upper-middle class white students in the universities who had worked with black people in ghettos and in voting drives in the South found themselves in the same situation. Students at universities in Berkeley, Columbia, Howard, Stanford, and Wisconsin raised fundamental questions concerning the value of the university and of what was being taught and militarization of the university. They described themselves as colonized. Marxists might see such self-description as entirely subjective and smacking of false consciousness. Nevertheless, the effects on the university of this consciousness during the 1960s and early 1970s was very great. It caused students to take and to be given more personal freedom. The subject matter and processes of teaching were reevaluated, and students were given powers which were hitherto undreamed of in universities in the United States. In many universities, students are involved in choosing the president, interviewing professors, and sitting on trustee boards. Whether any of this has had a significant effect is anoth⌐r question.

In the context of a time of economic instability and shrinking opportunities for children of the middle class, university students have become less adventuresome than in the 1960s. Many fear that they will lose their place in the middle class without any clearly worked out alternative life or means of assured economic stability. It was not until 1965 that the student movement and the civil rights movement became involved with the war in Indochina. The antiwar movement, which was highly decentralized, spontaneous, individualistic, and whiggish in attitude, grew each year from protest to forms of resistance. By late 1966, eight years before the end of the war, 50,000 to 100,000 people could be expected to turn out to march against the war in any of a half dozen major U.S. cities.

The antiwar movement served as a beacon to examine the national security state by forcing people to question the wisdom and prudence of its leaders. It caused the internationalist-minded to look with respect at men such as Robert Taft who asserted a noninterventionist road for the United States. U.S. leaders, Secretary of State Rusk once said, have always had to cajole and coerce Americans out of their isolationist lethargy and into an internationalist (imperialist) stance.[5] It was only a few years after Rusk made this statement that President Johnson was driven from office by this isolationist sentiment and the very set of ideals which he sought to reflect and coopt with the Great Society programs. One might add that Vance in his prudential approach appears to have drawn certain correct value conclusions from the recent tumultuous past.

Value shifts are often announced by poets and writers who recognize and promulgate cultural changes. This undertone is a yearning that they seek to bring into reality. Thus, the beat poets of the 1950s intended to proclaim a romantic vision which would serve as the basis for an alternative political program. Anyone familiar with Allen Ginsberg's writings understands the political coherence of his work and his attempts to present through action an alternative romantic vision which he thought could be quantified and used as a basis for a different life for the entire society. His poetic and yet practical lifestyle and the pragmatic anarchism of Paul Goodman attracted those who believed that an intellectually correct yet romantic and practical understanding of what was going on could be found, and together with that understanding, the process of a political alternative could be fashioned.

It is now the fashion to criticize the counterculture and its champions. Some have argued that it was merely the natural result of a consumer-oriented society which had lost the skill to work and the will to achieve. Its products and people were easily packaged and coopted by the corporate culture. Yet at its best, the counterculture was a last-ditch attempt to hold back an antihumanist thrust which was reflected in atomic bombs, soulless and impersonal architecture, and institutions of work and study which had become like jails. The counterculture led to a reevaluation of basic family life. Attempts were made to find meaning in the "small" and in principles of nondomination, and drugs were used to effect this kind of nirvana. Its residue of questioning and doubting authority remains, just as its assumptions are found in interests concerning the "small" and intermediate technology.

Perhaps the most powerful influence of the counter-culture relates to ways in which we now think about time and sexuality.

The corporate and national security culture organizes its major activities around "fast time," the number of revolutions per second, and paradoxically, an endless space which is to be politically controlled. Lives and activities are now broken into microseconds, be it the television commercial, the production line, the education test, or the laser beam in medical research. This mode of time efficiency and calculation is critical to the operations of the imperial and corporate enterprise which needs instant information and the transformation of human understandings of time into measureable amounts that can be successfully bought, sold, or charted on an efficiency chart. The ultimate and terrifying nature of this form of thought now manifests itself in the strategic and planning doctrines of the arms race in which the state is prepared to throw everyone into the funeral pyre and the planners of Armageddon shape SAC Minuteman warning systems to give the president an extra eight minutes to decide how to respond to an enemy missile attack.

It becomes a crucial political question to decide how the state can be confronted with radically different conceptions of time so that modern social organizations will bend to very different purposes (ones that are more in the realm of imagination than cognition). Part of such a discussion can invariably deteriorate into a "touchy-feely" set of ideas. Nevertheless, certain conceptions raised on the issues of sex and spirituality (concerns that involve a very different conception of time) are of a critical nature in bringing into being a culture which is strong enough to withstand the power of the national security state and imperialism. The out-of-favor Marxist Roger Garaudy has postulated the dialectic between the scholar and artisan, on the one hand, and the dancer artist, on the other. He argues that human existence can be best protected by seeing aesthetics as the ethics of the future. Aesthetics in this sense starts with the human experience as one which transcends techniques, utilitarian actions, and scientific puzzles. Thus, the restoration of the culture to its local everyday qualities becomes a means of confronting the Golem of state power.[7]

There is another crucial relationship dealing with the national security state and cultural mores which needs exploration. As in all states, U.S. officials use women as favors for foreign leaders. The usual reaction is one of puritanical shock or the amusement of the boulevardier, but another relationship between sexuality and politics is being explored in American culture. Wilhelm Reich believed that the repression of sexual needs results in the weakening of emotional functioning. This caused people to weaken in willpower, independence, and judgment. According to him, the authoritarian structures of fascism crippled people sexually and their fantasies came to rule them and forced them to seek perversions and embrace sexual assault as a means of engaging themselves with other human beings.

The American society is a very complicated and paradoxical one with regard to its sexual concerns. On the one hand, it is possible to analyze the pornography in various magazines including *Penthouse, Playboy,* and *Viva*—and different forms of sexual experimentation as merely a playing out of lusts which stem from authoritarian control.

Yet the changed attitudes toward sexuality have been linked to political changes that are reflected by and brought about by pornographic magazines. During 1970-71, impeachment charges were pressed by Gerald Ford in the House of Representatives against Justice William O. Douglas in part because of an article Douglas wrote that appeared in such a magazine. Douglas attacked the national security state as repressive. Several years later, Carter admitted to having lust in his heart in *Playboy*, and he is praised for his honesty by world leaders including Castro. Sexual liberation is now recognized and accepted as a political reality. This recognition generates relationships between men and women which tend toward equality and association rather than dependence and dominance. When feminists raise the banner of independence and rights, they promote the type of responsibility which rejects the repressive mechanisms of an authoritarian society and seek a more affirmative definition of moral obligation. Whether or not there is enough strength to work out the relationships between sexual liberation, family, and radical political transformation remains to be seen. A capitalist structure which seeks markets and packages all things and attributes is bound to applaud interactive relationships that are rootless and impermanent.

The issue of pornography also tends to raise the question of drugs and heightened consciousness. For purposes of analysis, it is important to see the role that all drugs play in the society to secure institutional quiet and pliancy and occupy all spaces including the inner life of an individual. Whether such drugs are legal or illegal is a secondary consideration to the epidemic of drug use in American society.

There is no doubt that certain forms of drugs are manipulated by institutional power to make people dumb and irresponsible. This is the way they are used in asylums, in schools, and by the police. The social control apparatus of the society has used drugs to protect the status quo and power relations in institutions. It was the national security state including the CIA and armed forces that encouraged the research and use of these drugs. It is naive to believe that these authoritarian institutions had no intention which they cared to implement. The intention was to control the lives and dreams of people. In this they achieved some success, just as liquor also had a controlling effect on industrial workers and thus buttressed the social status quo. Their success was that of the manipulators, just as a similar successful role of public relations people, advertising, and other forms of communications used for engineering consent is undeniable.

The change in the status and liberation of women through their own efforts has contributed to profoundly different sensibilities in life in the United States. Since the 1960s the arguments used by civil rights and student movement activists were used by women activists in describing their own deprived condition. While there is evidence to suggest that southern members of Congress attempted to sabotage the Civil Rights Act by including a prohibition against sexual discrimination, it is also true that congresswomen knew exactly what they were doing in rounding up support for it. Parallel to this direction was the establishment of status of women commissions in each state. As Jo Freeman has written in *Women's Liberation*: "These commissions were often urged by politically active women and were composed

primarily of women. While many governors saw
them as an easy opportunity to pay off political
favors, many women saw them as opportunities to
turn attention to their concerns."[8]

The idea of women's liberation was raised among
the student radical movement (SDS) in 1965 and
received no support from the men. For example, first
attempts at such change were presented by K.C.
Hayden, Tom Hayden's first wife, who pointed out the
atrocious behavior of men in the various activist
movements at about the time Congress added a sexual prohibition to the discrimination. Ideologically,
leftist men were as insensitive to women's demands
as was the rest of the society. It was not until 1969
that men had no choice but to become cognizant of the
large number of new groups concerning women's issues. Women saw themselves as independent of men
and able to organize wide-ranging support within the
middle class for their ideas of equality.

The women's movement will continue as a potentially explosive one both in the United States and
elsewhere because it goes to the very heart of social
organization, from the nature of the family to the
nature of the state. Within the United States, the
question is now being raised among the most advanced thinkers of how the economic and social organizations (for example, the corporations) must
change their values and goals as well as their patterns of work. Thus, the issue is not only discrimination per se but the nature of work and of organization
from a feminist point of view. This set of questions
will be taken up in other nations as well, whether
socialist or national liberationist.

The consumer movement in the United States
which dates back to the depression period did not

receive any massive support until it became clear in the 1960s that the corporations were making shoddy products with no apparent way for the customer to object. Political parties excluded concern with such matters from 1946 through 1964. Consumer goods became consumer "bads," and the sense of impotence and dependence on consumer goods was total. Ralph Nader has been the single most important person in the process of delegitimizing corporations and workers. He is a modern puritan who has developed a profound tactical and political sense of the institutional vulnerabilities of U.S. corporations. As a result of his work and those groups which he spawned, skepticism envelopes the corporation and its purposes in, for example, the automobile industry. New legislation has been passed on food and drugs as a result of consumer movement efforts, and workers have joined with various consumer groups to stop diseases such as black lung which are caused by poor conditions in the mines. But new legislation may only mean bureaucratic harrassment. It does not necessarily change conditions for the victims.

The delegitimation strategy of the consumer movement has not succeeded in changing the corporate structure. Consequently, it seeks alternatives. It has taken on a distinctly populist tone, favoring bureaucratic accountability, small cooperative enterprises, and an economic structure which would not be interwoven or dependent on the great corporations. This direction is dependent on the emergence of local and state leadership which is prepared to confront the great corporations in the towns and cities with laws which will bring on commerce.

The environmental movement in the United States stemmed from the view that Americans and U.S.

institutions were destroying nature at a rate which would make life unliveable without war. While the technological imperative of the United States was predicated on the importance of dominating nature, the insight of the radical environmentalists was that the means had to be found to live with nature. Thus, questions were asked about the kinds of chemicals which were made, the types of highways that were being developed, the quality of air which people had to breathe, and whether nuclear energy is both more dangerous and brings with it—under the guise of safety—more authoritarian social controls. These questions, central to the existence of any society, turned out to be profoundly distressing as workers in many places were told by corporations that high environmental standards were costing them their jobs. Thus, the environmental movement found itself battling against both workers and corporations. This crisis cannot be resolved through a bureaucratic balancing act because bureaucracies in their present state are part of the problem.

I have tried to suggest that these movements, which represented self-generated activity emerging from discontent and outrage, have had a profound effect on the American society. The Carter administration is working to incorporate or coopt the values reflected in these movements into the national security state. Until Carter's election, all presidents caught the lash of these movements and Congress itself is forced to question the methods of the state because of them.

But what about the other side of the spectrum in the United States? One is able to delineate certain tendencies. Parts of the national security apparatus remain under attack by Congress. Thus, the FBI, the

CIA, and NSA are now caught in a series of embarrassments over their past. What is disheartening, however, is that there is no real interest in the Carter administration or organized interest groups that challenge the basic charters of these organizations. Liberal members of Congress, such as Kennedy and Kastenmeier, find that the Department of Justice under Griffin Bell is far more open to the complaints of the CIA and FBI than was the case under his predecessor, Edward Levi. Indeed, Carter ordered joint working groups of the CIA, FBI, and Justice Department to draft new regulations that would give the color of law to previously sanctioned but illegal activity.

Even with the Carter administration, there is a period of deadlock and waiting concerning the political and economic direction the United States will take over the next twenty years. The ability of the United States to straddle fascism and socialism in its economic and political organization remains the basic problem of the national security state as Carter attempts to dance between the two with his brand of symbol manipulation.

While Carter and his group have coopted opposition to the state, the fundamental structural problems deepen. The liberal politicians of the Democratic Party recognize deep class, race, and economic divisions within the United States that frighten the more responsible of them. This is one reason party leadership is prepared to rally around presidential leadership seeking personal gain as the alternative to structural change. For the first time since 1948, issues concerning the nature of the United States as a class society will be consistently raised in federal politics but not necessarily as progressive issues.

Most politicians are campaigning against the poor
and are prepared to accept high employment rates.
(At present, the overall rate of employment in the
United States is 6 percent while it is as high as 17
percent in major cities.) Others, such as the labor
coalitions, seek to restore the Roosevelt magic in the
hopes of saving New Deal capitalism while Republicans such as Reagan are prepared to further fortify
the power of the police and the military. They believe
that there has been too much liberty and permissive-
ness in the United States. What the American people
need, according to this point of view, is a good authoritarian spanking of the kind which former Vice-
President Agnew prescribed. The ideas of the Left
remain the most vital and the most likely to have a
long-term effect on the American people. However,
this effect cannot take hold until these ideas and
consciousness are translated into specific programs
and political organization. Whether this will occur
remains to be seen.

What are our conclusions? We have accepted the
idea that the national security state was "necessary"
to obtain the passive allegiance of the people. The
national security state was also absolutely crucial for
the development of the empire in that it rationalized
decisions, it organized planning strategies for controlling different countries, and it developed an
ideology of sophisticated and self-delusional manipulation as a means for the acceptance of open-ended
imperial commitment through secrecy, loyalty, research grants, and need-to-know standards. It made
practical Reinhold Niebuhr's vested interest in the
belief that the interpersonal morality of no lies,
cheating, or murders was a luxury when publicly
applied. Its military and bureaucratic leadership op-

erated in the framework of organizational continuity to ensure the assumptions of the various services and the assumptions of collective organization against communism.

From Peru to Portugal, from South Korea to Indochina and to Berlin and Israel, the assumption of the U.S. protectorates that the United States would be prepared to go to war there or could control those areas through its culture, corporations, or military are now under severe scrutiny and actual attack. While attempts were made to "make nice" by Colby, Kissinger, Schlesinger, Kelley, and now Carter's group, the Trilateral Commission, the *raison d'etre* of the national security state is shaken. The empire abroad is shaken, and its domestic underpinnings are therefore loosened. The reason for its existence will become less obvious.

Nevertheless, as Borosage and I have pointed out, the possibilities of preparing legislation and organizing groups to support particular pieces of legislation which would lead to the dismantlement of the national security apparatus instead of to the legitimation of secret decision making or covert intervention is unlikely. There is the legitimation process of paralaw so that what was once considered illegal and criminal is given the status of legality and legitimacy. Actions which the state once performed in the night end up being shown on television because they are anointed as legal with the full panoply of the law as the cover for otherwise outrageous actions. When this system of legitimation is either questioned or interrupted, there are marches of FBI agents who serve notice that the bureau is a political force as strong as the CIA. The Congress itself, for all its faults and its present tendency toward conservatism, stands somewhat outside the state apparatus because it has its roots in the people. Its strength, as is the case with any representative body, is the willingness of the representative to both represent and hold a dialogue with the people. Those of us involved in political education can only attack the national security apparatus effectively through the process of dialogue concerning the state itself and its relationship to a basic understanding of human creative possibility. Once we have dialogues in our communities about such issues, and we find a series of slogans which relate to our dialogues, we are able to help the society at large including the four million people stuck in the imperial and oppressor assumptions of the national security state.

The work of the national security state is based on mythicizing people, who they are and what they do. How else can we explain the willingness of leaders and followers to develop genocidal systems of defense in the name of protecting the so-called free world against communism? The task of dialogue with those operating according to particular roles of the state is to break the categories from which they would judge the world. The effect of the various social movements of the last fifteen years has been to demythicize people and force dialogue among those who refused to see one another except as abstract entities.

Within the United States, the media is authority-oriented. It will invariably cover and work with power against the powerless. In this process, it has also developed its own power which is a kind of transient interest in anything. This transient interest in any issue also implies that it seeks fashion. It is bored with discussions of systemic questions. This does not mean that we have a media which seeks to represent the people to power. It does mean that it is an instrument in any battle against fascism because journalists, by the nature of their work, must gossip and thus be opposed to secrecy. Perhaps the media will see its adversary interest as it seeks privileges of confidentiality which it insisted President Nixon did not have. But to seek privileges for the media *estate* is not the same as changing the national security state.

The third issue presented was the consumer choice in the national security state. Economic growth in capitalism seeks the production of a plethora of consumer goods and leisure services, but the cultural changes of the last decade confront the whole issue of consumerism in ways which one would not have thought possible a decade ago. The task Carter faces is to manipulate the growing disenchantment with consumer goods to a political acceptance of the status quo. Paradoxically, the mass consciousness of the society must continue to accept the belief that consumer choice is the true meaning of democracy. This belief can be sustained only if the Democratic Party and the liberals within it commit themselves to top-down planning for social welfare, health insurance, energy conservation, consumer production, and armaments with the great corporations. There is little to suggest that they are going to be successful in this objective because it will appear to be too liberal. It would require the candidacy of Ted Kennedy against Carter, and therefore the South and Southwest of the Democratic Party.

There is another profound tension in the national security state itself. It is the reassertion of capitalist definitions of value in defense. There remains no objective obtained or sought which is equal to the dollar costs of the present defense system. Capitalism is interminably in search of value, equivalence, and how to get its money's worth. The ideology of the national security state is that there is no such thing as a money's worth equivalence to national security or defense. As a defense budget becomes more grandiose and it becomes clearer that local capitalists have limits on spending, reordering could result.

There is another important consideration. The American people have not participated in the national security state except as objects and financial donors to it. Imperial slogans of another generation are now judged harshly as independent citizens lose their belief in the national security state, and members of the state seek new missions and purposes. National security, as presently defined, is irrelevant to them in their understanding of what their lives are and what they hope to achieve. This means that people in and outside of government are far more open to an alternative program which will take the best of what we have learned from the past and relate that to our needs and understanding of new possibilities. Such a program will surely be built on techniques of persuasion, confrontation, and cooperation with and including different elements of the national security state.

Of course, even then we do not know whether positive social transformation will occur. Albert Szent Gyorgi once said that the only real way to change is to have the rulers die out. It is only the next generation which will save us because it is bored with the thoughts and fears of their parents. I think his view is a bit too pessimistic. We are in the grip of profound changes which in turn enlarges political debate and changes its focus. We will see natural and healthy antagonisms emerge which will cause the state structure to change under the influence of a new generation and terrible, irresolvable problems.

However, healthy directions can occur only if there is an exercise of political and rational will which seeks to withdraw people from the assumptions of imperialism and the national security state. This can be accomplished through organizing a political dialogue of disaffiliation and affirmation. Cities, local officials, universities, and bureaucracies could be engaged in comprehending how the organizational purposes and forms of the national security state and its twin, the great corporation, have made humane purposes their enemy. As a result, the process of disaffiliation must begin. But what is to be reaffirmed? The process of reaffirmation begins with recognizing that dialogues can lead to a clarity of program and method among those who have comprehended their own impotence and colonization but who have not yet made the connection between their situation and the violent and oppressive assumptions of the national security state. The way in which we can help to uncover and act on this connection is our political and cultural task in the amazing twentieth century's remaining years.

NOTES

1. Stockholm International Peace Research Institute, *World Armaments and Disarmament Yearbook* (1975) p. 144.

2. James Tobin, "On the Economic Burden of Defense," in *Defense, Science and Public Policy*, ed. Edwin Mansfield (New York: W.W. Norton, 1968), pp. 34-35.

3. Ibid.

4. Martin Luther King statement in 1962; as quoted in Herbert von Borch, *The Unfinished Society* (New York: Hawthorn Books, Inc., Publishers, 1962), p. 162.

5. Richard John Neuhaus, "The Thorough Revolutionary," in Peter L. Berger and Richard John Neuhaus, *Movement and Revolution* (New York: Doubleday-Anchor, 1970), p. 140.

6. Dean Rusk as quoted in Henry F. Graff, *The Tuesday Cabinet* (New York: Prentice-Hall, 1970), p. 135.

7. *Allen Verbatim: Lectures on Poetry, Politics, Consciousness*, ed. Gordon Ball (New York: McGraw-Hill Book Co., 1974); Paul Goodman, *New Reformation: Notes of a Neolithic Conservative* (New York: Random House, 1970).

8. Roger Garaudy, *An Alternative Future: A Vision of Christian Marxism* (New York: Simon and Schuster, 1974), pp. 121-45.

9. Jo Freeman, *The Politics of Women's Liberation: A Case Study of an Emerging Social Movement and Its Relation to the Policy Process* (New York: David McKay, Co., Inc., 1975), p. 52.

10. Casey Hayden and Mary King, "A Kind of Memo," circulated in 1965 and published as "Sex and Caste: A Kind of Memo" in *Liberation* 11 (1965): 35; noted in Jo Freeman, p. 57.

Index